C000018532

BUSINESS MELTDOWN

How Development is Killing Business

Andrea McNeil

 Andrea McNeil is an Entrepreneur, Author and Speaker. She owns The Headspace Company, a non-development, non-training, non-coaching organisation specialising in creating outstanding leaders.

CONTENTS

PART ONE: BUSINESS MELTDOWN

One cannot teach a man anything. One can
only enable him to learn from within himself.

Galileo Galilei (1564-1642)

Businesses, HR departments and individuals are driven by the incorrect belief that if they identify and fix gaps in skills, knowledge or capability, they will have found the magic solution to creating a great leader.

Reliance on self-help courses, leadership development programmes and psychometric assessments does nothing to enable you to build more resilience, become more creative and make better decisions. In fact, these interventions work against the very things you are trying to change.

Millions of pounds and thousands of hours are wasted applying tests, concepts and theories to the never-ending need to learn more, do better and grow faster.

The reality is all this effort is wasted.

Have you noticed that, despite all the research, new models and current theories, the gaps are still there? Why do the 'issues' which need resolving and the missing leadership talents remain a problem?

All the extraneous analysis, concept understanding and hand-wringing over how to implement this knowledge in day-to-day life, does nothing more than add further overwhelm and stress in the long term.

It's like putting a plaster on your finger to tackle a chronic disease.

WHAT'S BUSINESS MELTDOWN?

Warning of a business meltdown is a dramatic, attention-grabbing statement.

I chose the title deliberately to give a very loud, very real wake-up call to those in business.

For the last few years, I've followed the research of thought leaders who have been predicting risks facing businesses. From the raft of unexpected losses suffered by many of the UK's longest-standing, most successful companies, there are lessons we can learn which helps head them off for other businesses.

The potential changes to businesses over the next decade appear overwhelming.

Consider:

- The rise in technology and the 24/7 information-rich world we have access to.
- The shift in access to education and pools of talent to new, developing nations.
- The emergence of new, economically expanding nations such as Brazil, India and China.
- Changes in how we live and the environments we work in, leading to more isolated, virtual working.

WHY BUSINESSES NEED TO CHANGE

For you, as a business leader and an individual, these global factors already have an impact on how you feel and behave. The reality is, to be able to deal with this incredible pace of change, some fundamental shifts in our thinking are needed.

Now, we must:

- Embrace instability, and become 'built for flux'.
- Enjoy re-designing, adapting and creating solutions to complex problems.
- Bring more creativity into your time and your organisation.
- Encourage innovation. Fast.
- Get used to 'not knowing'. Learn to deal with ambiguity.
- Decrease reliance on hierarchy and build greater reliance

on self-managed teams.
- Be open minded, developing new ways to inject fresh thinking.
- Encourage entrepreneurial thinking.
- Build a future focus. Attempting to replicate what worked yesterday, will leave you vulnerable today.

WHY BUSINESS LEADERS NEED TO WAKE UP

Whilst these future challenges are real, for many in business today, there are issues in need of immediate attention.

A lot of media attention is focused on the need to free up capital and encourage business growth to support the slow exit out of the global recession. There's so much emphasis on the development of systems and processes to ensure any business can run smoothly within whatever commercial market it operates.

From my time working both in businesses and with businesses, there's much discussion over what every business needs to do or know, to cope with current and future challenges.

Here are some common traits you'll see business publications naming as essential to grow your business and create success.

- Identify and develop talent, from diverse and often declining sources.
- Access creativity and innovation to 'stay ahead' of the competition.
- Improve problem-solving and better decision-making, in

the face of an abundance of information and the need to find consensus.

- Develop engaged employees, who thrive on positivity and who can deal with workplace conflict through improved communication skills.
- Develop a positive mindset.
- Grow new skills and capabilities to deal with new demands in your role.

So what?!

I can guarantee you these traits - along with many others - have been on the 'must do' list of HR directors and business leaders for many, many years. The exact words may not be the same or as 'corporate', but you'll recognise these more commonly as the:

- Need to deal with others more effectively.
- Need to understand yourself better.
- Need to manage stress and feelings of overwhelm better.
- Need to get more done in less time.
- Need to act instead of procrastinating.

As you can see, it's a significant list and one which has been around for a number of years. It focuses on what you as an individual must do to protect yourself from failure.

This is where the risk of business meltdown is at its greatest.

The core of any business is not the systems or processes; it is the people who work within it. Any business, from 'solo-preneur' and SME, to large corporate, is currently facing meltdown due to the challenges facing its people.

Starting with the individual, the demands placed upon each of you right now are immense.

You are expected to deal with vast quantities of information, deal with a range of tasks at any one time and still have the capacity to build effective relationships with those around you. Today, you each 'know' more than ever and in many ways 'do' more than ever (even if it's just watching TV).

In any business, the owner, manager or leader must fulfil a raft of expectations and tasks to 'do well'. They must somehow create strategies for the future when the future is unclear and unpredictable. They're required to master the mechanics of social media, marketing and selling, even when these aren't obviously linked to their role. They need to understand how customers tick; what it takes to engage employees; deliver the day job and cope with leading constant change.

Apparently though, all is not lost.

For every skill, behaviour or task to be mastered, there are ways development can help. For the individual, development comes in the form of self-help books, meditation skills, weekend mindfulness retreats or personal development programmes

For businesses, there is an abundance of management theories, leadership frameworks, psychometric assessments and talent development programmes. All of which are designed to provide the insight, skills and development methods to fill the skills gaps of employees and leaders. One feature of these development programmes is the need to measure, analyse and judge. In this way they help determine the level of performance, the likely impact of change and track success.

You may have experienced measurement methods like these:

- An assessment questionnaire, answered by yourself or by others about you.
- A series of reflective questions provided at the end of each piece of key learning.
- Feedback, either formal feedback through anonymous questionnaires and ratings, or informal feedback through asking others about the experience of working together.
- Profiling, often used as a follow up to feedback or questionnaires, where your answers are deepened and checked, creating a fuller picture of who you are; your traits; how you operate, often in comparison with others.

We're led to believe these traits or development needs are something to be sought, developed, learned and aspired to in some way. For many, their progress is managed, controlled, monitored, then rewarded or punished through very public performance management processes.

It has created an industry for developing leaders, developing managers, developing personal effectiveness and so on. The problem is these very programmes are only adding to the overwhelm, fear of failure and lists of things to do for already over-burdened people.

Permeating this industry is the never-ending sense there's always something more to learn or do differently.

The belief that by mastering a new set of skills or by managing time better, you'll perform better, feel better or deliver more for your business, is ill-founded, at best. What's worse is the expectation that each model or theory has the answer, putting even greater pressure on the individual if they can't achieve the expected results.

Business meltdown is already here.

People in business are already stuck in a cycle of self-analysis, feedback, identification of weaknesses and an approach to 'fill the gap'.

To me, the pressure to succeed, to overcome weaknesses and develop new strategies to cope, is limiting the capacity of people to perform at their best. In my view, these interventions are using up time, energy and resource with little lasting effects.

On a personal level, I've experienced the excitement when I've found a great, new self-help book which shouts at me to read it, promising 'the answer'. I've been down the road of avoiding such books and deciding instead to 'empty my mind' through meditation. Even this left me wondering why I couldn't meditate 'properly' and feeling frustrated by the endless thoughts filling my head. Somehow, I believed I could never find the answer to being stressed until I had mastered this meditative state.

Wrong!!

Step back a minute

If any of this sounds familiar, you're in the right place. There is a way to head off the meltdown.

I expect right now, you're asking some very sensible questions:

How can all these development experts be wrong?

How can all these theories, models and processes be of no value?

You may have personally experienced good results from the understanding gained and changes implemented through a personal development process.

But let me ask you this:

- How long did the awareness last?
- How effective were the changes over a longer period of time?
- Do you really feel free of the need to fix, control and develop?

Based on my own experience, my guess is, you'll certainly enjoy the fruits of new understanding and new awareness, in the short term at least.

Back to my meditating example, I absolutely realised how beneficial it was to stop, take time out of my day and attempt to clear my mind. However, it was clear by 'doing' meditation, I was also adding to my daily task list and was actually getting hung up on the need to get it 'right'.

Of course, for some people, some of the time, personal development may lead to a degree of breakthrough.

Remember this, though, a broken clock will also look like it tells the correct time twice a day.

Does that mean the clock works?

Fundamentally, to get the correct time, you don't simply move the hands, you go to the core mechanics and see what's broken. Once we're able to see the core, true mechanics of how we operate, we're then able use any of these additional models to provide guidance and fine tune our way of being.

WHAT'S IT ALL ABOUT?

I was compelled to write this book to shake up the traditional views on how people learn, grow and change. For over 20 years, I've been in the world of learning and development, both in corporate roles and as a freelance development professional.

Over that time, I've been a leader, a business owner and I've been trained in many approaches to self and leadership development. I have worked as a coach for the last 10 years and jumped on the roundabout of awareness-raising, insight development and change.

When I realised I was getting nowhere, I knew it was time to get off and find another way to get to the source of creativity, authenticity and clear-thinking. I had experienced that same repetitive cycle and found myself still looking for the answer. Here I share my own shift in understanding and how it has influenced this book.

MY DEVELOPMENT JOURNEY

As a 'development professional', I've been through my fair share of self- development programmes, as well as creating them for business leaders.

Despite a great deal of self-analysis, reflection, awareness raising and development of new behaviours, I found myself struggling with the demands on me as a business owner. I've always been keen to discover more, very aware of my weaknesses and constantly striving for perfection.

Why then could I still not get things right?

Why did I struggle to balance competing demands, expectations and still remain true to myself?

For years, the more I tried to find the answers to these questions, the more I created a head full of thoughts, fears and possibilities. I became the 'person who thinks too much'.

I'd wake up in the night, reflecting on events from the day before and predicting many possible scenarios for the days ahead. I was exhausted by the time and energy I spent in this cycle. Yet, it still never seemed to help me find the answers I was looking for.

Finally, something changed. I started to notice my thoughts and the feelings they created. And I came to understand a few fundamentals truths:

- I was the only one creating these thoughts.
- I was experiencing my thoughts, not the circumstances of my life.
- At any time I could choose which thoughts to follow, which to watch drift away and I alone have the capacity to allow my thoughts to change.
- When I let go of trying to manage and control events around me, I could tune into my instincts.
- Living life more in the moment - not based on past experiences or future possibilities - gave me the headspace to think clearly and make better decisions.
- I was working very hard at my life, trying to drive myself towards solutions, when all I needed was to turn around, stop pushing and find the natural re-balancing which was always available to me.

And these have freed me from my own personal meltdowns.

Now read this book to show you where traditional approaches to self- development come unstuck. It will give you an understanding of where to look for the only way to bring about the changes you and your business need.

HOW TO READ THIS BOOK

In writing this book, I've explored some of the common leadership development models I've worked with over my years in business. I want to provide an overview of development focus for each one. Then I'll explain why each one will never prevent the meltdown you must strive to avoid.

I started writing this book as a helpful summary of everything I had learned in my years as a developer of people and leaders. I wanted to sprinkle in a fair few theories and facts to help you understand the road you're on and the next steps in your journey to be a better leader.

I've had this desire to enable people to find their true potential and free themselves from the paralysis created by the pace of change, the over-abundance of information and the uncertainties we all face.

From my work in business, I could clearly see the 'corporate malaise' facing so many businesses, arising from poor decision-making, lack of accountability, and lack of actions or results. All this leads to a gradual stagnation of self-belief, reduced creativity and lack of clarity in thought and action.

As the development of the book progressed I realised it wasn't enough to look at the impact of development on individuals. Every business is underpinned by one essential factor: the success of relationships.

When you are trying to develop, resolve issues or change something about yourself, you are impacted by the people around you. Business meltdown will come from individuals and teams, so it's important to include relationship development in this review.

The aim of this book is not to develop a new prescriptive leadership model to 'fix all' and offer the next big idea for self-improvement and development. In fact, it's quite the opposite.

Right now to head off meltdown, everyone needs something different: they need flexibility, agility, responsiveness and a good healthy dose of 'not knowing'.

Whether you are in a leadership role or not, I suggest you look at yourself in a completely different way. You simply need to turn around and shift your focus from trying to master the effects of the events and circumstances around you and, instead, start to tune into yourself and your innate wisdom.

I want this book to challenge you and your thinking:

- How clear are you about how you, your thoughts and emotions affect others?
- What happens when the going gets tough, when you find your stress levels building and your emotions running high?
- How well do you know what's going on within yourself and how this, in turn, affects others around you?
- How do emotions affect your ability to deal with what's in front of you, as well as finding solutions to problems of which you've only just become aware?

You don't exist in a bubble.

Everything you know, believe or feel yourself to be, inherently impacts everyone around you. In every exchange, team or group setting you're in a relationship with someone else. You are part of a living, breathing, dynamic system connecting each and every one of us.

I want this book to have you look for answers to these questions in completely different places. To do this, I ask you keep an open mind and allow yourself to go with the flow. Figuring out and creating judgements are not required!

PART TWO: UNDERSTAND YOURSELF

What we pay attention to and how we pay attention determines the content and quality of life.

Mihaly Csikszentmihalvi (2003)

INTRODUCTION

There are legions of models, frameworks and processes available to us, all created to help us understand who we are, how we tick and what we need to develop.

The need to understand more about what makes you what you are encompasses the work of counsellors, psychologists and therapists, as well as workplace development specialists.

I'm sure if you're reading this book you have spent time and money researching, developing and practising the skills and behaviours necessary to counteract some part of you, which seems to be getting in the way of your success or happiness.

The self-help industry is almost as vast as the diet industry, so there's clearly a widespread perceived need out there.

Once you enter the business arena, the need to uncover your strengths and weaknesses is magnified even further. Measuring you for capabilities, skills and behaviours, alongside analysis of your personality traits, has become common place in most organisations. By attempting to add scientific rigour to the intangible world of behaviours and attitude, gives most businesses the reassurance that they are on the right track to recruit and develop the best employees.

Even my 18 year old son, as he tried to enter the world of simple Saturday work, had to navigate a fair few online psychometric and personality questionnaires, before any kind of face-to-face interaction was offered.

Progressing within a business requires the development of new, broader or deeper capabilities, designed to reflect the new responsibilities of each new role.

Once you get into the management or leadership levels - or are simply identified as someone who will be rising to a leadership role soon - you notice a raft of assessment, development planning, competency measuring and interventions, designed to help you become better at what you do and who you are.

Even if you're running your own business, you cannot escape the pervading sense you're doing something wrong.

You'll have gone from being a specialist in a service, such as plumber, accountant or printer, and all too soon the drive to scale your business has you hooked into the need to know more and do more. I've experienced this shift, at a most basic level, when I realised I needed to become more adept at marketing and selling.

If you add to this the next step of managing/leading staff and suppliers, you're layering in a whole new set of expectations and potential deficiencies. Now, as an individual or business owner, you'll not have a whole HR department to set up the processes and guidelines, against which you can assess and develop yourself. So, typically, you'll find your own way.

You'll hear about development programmes from your peers; you'll see others who come back from an intensive weekend course with a whole new attitude. And you'll feel you want some.

Even something as common-place as wanting to change something about your business will move you to investigate further what you need to do or know to make the change.

You'll hire in some external expert who has managed change before and who you feel can show you the best way forward and reduce the risk of disaster with your people, processes or systems.

Don't get me wrong; it's great we want to develop and broaden our skills, behaviours and knowledge. I'm not suggesting any of the self-development books and programmes will do you harm or are a complete waste of time. I'm also not, by any stretch of the imagination, telling you not to develop as a person, manager or leader.

What you need to do is let go for the belief that any or all of these approaches will 'fix you'. Holding on to this belief only perpetuates the problem and will move you closer to meltdown. The endless cycle of analysis, planning and development strategies creates distraction and more action plans than you can ever deliver. Multiply this across a number of employees and you have a business in severe danger of over-heating and losing focus.

What I ask you to do is stop for a little while and soak in something quite amazing:

To understand and develop yourself, you don't need to know more, do more or change who you are.

HOW TO GET THE MOST FROM THIS SECTION

In this next section, I'll take you through some of the building blocks we need to help us function as the best people and leaders we can be. We'll go on a little tour of some great leadership and development models I've come across and used with clients in the past.

We'll then stop and look in a completely different place which will change your understanding of how you can develop all you need and stop wasting so much time and energy relying on processes which never fully get you to where you want to be.

By now, you may start to realise this book aims to offer you something different from the typical 'leadership development' perspective.

Sure, I'll bring in lots of examples of theories and writers who may be familiar to you. However, it feels to me most business leaders just don't need any more of the same to deal with the challenges they face today. These examples will by no means be a complete review of their approach or theory. If you want to know more about each, I've included a reference, so you can delve deeper yourself.

If you're like me, you're looking for something different from just 'knowing more'.

You're looking for something which will fundamentally change the way you operate and how you are 'being' in the world.

This doesn't mean you'll get some naval-gazing exercise in self-enlightenment (which, by the way, has its place in achieving time-out and refection). Rather, in this book, I hope you'll start to develop your own understanding of what you already know and use this to shift to get where you want to be.

So, before you start this section, I'd like you to clear your head of any preconceptions about what is to follow.

You'll find a way to move away from reactive, emotional, 'outside in' thinking. This will lead you to greater agility, responsiveness and flexibility, along with a good healthy dose of 'not knowing'.

Notice how this feels as you read it and then let go. You have already started 'not knowing' by reading this book.

CHAPTER ONE:
BEGINNING WITH YOU

It would have been easy to start a book on business meltdown by looking at all the business strategies, plans and processes putting a strain on the successful functioning of any business. I guess that's what a lot of business books do.

With any business you need to start with the core elements holding it all together. This place is with every individual, each one who makes up a cog in the wheel or a part of the jigsaw.

Interestingly, the concept of meltdown is something I've seen frequently applied to people rather than business. Even in the 80's and 90's when I entered the corporate world, it was full of over-worked, burnt-out workers who had simply reached the end point and had a meltdown, often publicly, and with catastrophic effects.

In the last few years of tough economic times and increasing pace of change, I've seen an increasing number of people struggle to apply old ways to new challenges, resulting in some pretty stressful outcomes.

Of course, when people in business are experiencing meltdown, the business will be in meltdown too. This comes from an over-reliance on new, company-wide methods brought in to solve the 'people problem'. As soon as a business starts looking outside for the solution, the very approaches brought into help will create more problems.

People become engrossed in adhering to change plans or how their performance measures up against others, to the point where they lose sight of their own innate abilities and talents. However, when beginning to understand one's self, as an adult, we've always been encouraged to try to understand more about who we are, in our own right.

It's a tough ask to understand yourself, when you actually live and breathe every day without even thinking about who you are.

As a result, we hand over the power to assess, measure and reflect back on ourselves, to others. Many leadership and development theories rely on this as a way of helping us see our characteristics and behaviours more clearly.

So, I'm going to strip this away for the moment and request you to stop and ask yourself:

WHO ARE YOU?

I wonder if, by this point in your life, when you stop and reflect on this question, you have clear sight of who you are. If it's a bit muddied and not as concrete as you thought, don't worry, it's completely natural.

As you progress through life, your sense of who you are will be influenced, molded and changed through your experiences.

Most of these experiences are picked up from things that happen around you or to you, such as how you are brought up, what happened at school and how you developed during your work life. So much of what you believe about yourself is likely to have come from what you've heard others say about you.

Those experiences and events are stored in the brain as mental maps and used by your brain to help you deal with new thoughts, situations and events every day. For many, it would seem like a standard, efficient process by which we all grow and develop into the adults we have become.

The reality for many, however, is very different. Some individuals - myself included - have realised the old stories about who we are and what we can do, are just that... stories.

These stories have been made up by others (or ourselves) in response to external circumstances over which we feel we have no control. As familiar as these stories are, and in spite of the perceived safety they provide, you feel maybe the story doesn't quite fit. It feels like you're struggling along in an ill-fitting jacket.

Maybe the 'jacket' belongs to someone else and is restricting who you are, how you show up in the world and who you want to become.

This book aims to help you shed this ill-fitting jacket, to create the space to move more freely and create what's needed for you to be at your authentic best.

Right now, I can hear you say:

"That's all very well if the pace of life wasn't moving so fast. I can barely stop to breathe or think, let alone check the 'jacket' I'm wearing."

If this sounds like you, you're in the right place. What you'll find here will help you shed the layers and create everything you need to deal with the world, today and tomorrow.

In the field of development, it's common to make assumptions about what's tough, demanding and stressful in life, both at work or at home. Naturally, individuals don't react to the same pressures in the same way.

Before we step into the world of development theories, which attempt to assess how you deal with challenging situations, here's a question for you:

HOW ARE YOU DEALING WITH THE INCREASED DEMANDS IN LIFE?

What do you do every day?

You get a feeling in the pit of your stomach every day when you open your emails and try to stay on top of everything you must remember and the problems you need to solve.

Remembering, solving and processing are hugely draining and require you to be in a 'doing' mode all day. You continually draw on your mental maps of past experiences to help you find the way through.

Every email, every piece of information, every interaction creates a series of thoughts and feelings. Our physiology makes you attempt to store all of this in your short term memory in the belief you can make sense of it all and take action. Unfortunately, it's unlikely to be successful.

Our short term memory has a very limited capacity and struggles when you try to hold information this way. To free capacity and processing power, neuroscientists (researchers who study how our brains work) advise writing down or creating images of what we need to deal with. This frees up headspace.

There's a lot of 'doing' involved, even in something as natural as thinking this way. Throughout the day your energy levels reduce as you keep drawing on the limited reserves in your brain.

No wonder so many of us feel so tired at the end of each day, even if we're just sat in an office. Our brains experience a more rigorous workout than our bodies.

What do you already know?

To get through this mental exhaustion, there's certain physiological processes which kick in automatically. For example, you may notice surges of adrenalin through the day, which over time become expected and feel essential for survival.

When the surge lapses you feel exhausted and, chances are, it occurs right in the middle of something you consider to be important at the time. You'll look for another fix, to give you a boost of energy, to re-fuel your brain and get you over the next hurdle.

In this state, you're constantly looking for answers around you:

- Does someone know more than you?
- Why are they clear about the future when you're not?
- How do they achieve their goals, when your goals are constantly changing?

You're aware of many people who seem to have it sussed.

Interestingly, you also already know of ways to successfully manage the chaos and disturbance which emerges during certain points in your life. You will have successfully navigated multitudes of tasks at the same time. You will embark on journeys where you really aren't sure of the outcome or what to do.

Take, for example, becoming a parent. You may have become a parent deliberately or accidentally, but when the baby arrives you instinctively know what to do.

Ironically, you're more likely to become confused and overwhelmed when you start reading books and theories, telling you 'the best way' to parent. You'll likely get together with other parents or health professionals, and start to hear about how they manage and what they believe is 'the best way'.

It's often at this point a parent who instinctively knows what to do, starts believing they are useless or don't know enough, adding to feel they are failing. They have become disconnected from their natural state of being a parent and start to follow others.

What stops you connecting to your being?

What's happened is the 'reality' created by all the experts and people around you have clouded your own instinctive wisdom. When this happens, you stop being able to hear what your instinct is telling you and your brain generates patterns of thought which create feelings of stress, unhappiness and overwhelm.

Typically, you react to these feelings by trying to know more, finding a different solution and often think you need to 'go deeper' to fix the issue. In fact, when this happens, you are looking in the wrong place.

Adding more knowledge taken from the outside world and adding more methodical problem-solving takes you away from the place you need to be. This place is right inside you, the place where you already have all the understanding, knowledge and skills you need.

When you turn down the volume on your thinking, create a little space and notice, you'll hear the answer. It often manifests itself as a 'blurt' or an 'aha' moment or a feeling deep down something is right. It's here your instinctive wisdom has space to come to the fore.

When this wisdom has the space to breathe and flourish, you will make better decisions more quickly, be more instinctively creative and find greater balance in your work and home life.

Where to look?

The range of leadership models can be daunting. Added to this, there's a constant cycle of development, which seems to create a new model every few years. It's not easy to work out what you should be doing, what model you should be following and what you need as a leader.

In this part of the book, you'll discover what's happening to you and millions of others who feel the same way you do, who may be looking in the wrong place to find the answers to the challenges you face.

I'll take you through a number of perspectives to increase your understanding of how things work. This will help find a way to make changes which work for you. These perspectives demonstrate how different frameworks and theories help you change your thinking and increase your awareness of how you and others tick.

Where to look will become clear. It's not 'out there', it's inside yourself.

Now read on to find out what I mean by this...

FOUNDATIONS OF SUCCESS

To streamline the journey of understanding I've focused on the key elements generally believed to be essential for success. The theory goes that if you follow the development models described for each of these, you'll prevent personal meltdown and maximise your performance. As we all know, better individual performance leads to better business performance, so avoiding business meltdown.

These foundational elements are:

- Trust
- Authenticity
- Adaptability
- Decision-making
- Dealing with competing demands
- Emotional intelligence

This section looks at each of these elements, both in terms of traditional theories and models used to explain each and presenting an alternative view. No one wants development interventions to kill business or create meltdown, I'll show you how this risk can be reduced.

CHAPTER TWO:
HOW YOUR MIND WORKS

Many people I've worked with recently have linked their struggles with operating effectively in business, with the stress and anxiety created by the demands of working life. In particular, I've seen an increase in companies asking for training programmes on resilience.

It sounds serious to me and I'm not sure training people on resilience can be effective in any way, apart from telling them they need to be aware of the need for it.

Recently, I ran a workshop to help business leaders deal with their sense of overwhelm, created by the 24/7 information stream and the exhaustion that can set in through the working day.

At the time, I was curious about how humans are designed to deal with information demands and the high level of mental processing required in the 21st Century. In developing these workshops, I researched how the brain works and how it impacts how the mind is or isn't able to deal with the tasks it is given.

It struck me that when you're trying to learn a new skill how something works, it's always good to understand how something works and why it is made to work the way it does.

For example, if you want to understand how to do a perfect press up, understand why a move or the placement of an arm has an impact on how well the exercise is completed. I recognise that for some people, just being told is enough, but for me, I always felt instructions for improving the skill always made more sense when the 'why' behind the 'how' was clear.

Following this, I wanted to devote space to provide an overview of how your brain works and why your mind impacts you the way it does.

The good news is you don't have to be a neuroscientist to understand how parts of your brain work together and how these impact your thinking, feeling and behaviours. Our minds have a powerful influence on much of what we do, how we feel and the patterns we live by. At various points, I'll explain what it means in practice when you come up against some of life's challenges. I'll show you how the power of your mind can be harnessed in different ways to help you achieve better results, make decisions quicker and find clarity in your thinking.

One of the best descriptions about how your brain is structured and how it works, was described by Dr Steve Peters in his book The Chimp Paradox[1]. Peters is a sports psychologist who worked with many Olympic gold medal winners over the years.

He simplifies the brain into a system of seven brains and created a working model of the mind based on three of these seven brains – the Parietal, the Frontal and the Limbic brain, which together create your Psychological Mind.

Typically, these three brains work together to help you function. However, at times they work in opposition, which creates an inner struggle for control and a sense of conflict in your mind.

Peters describes the frontal part of your brain as the 'Human brain', which he labels as 'you'. In this part of the brain, the frontal (or human) area creates thoughts, processes information and develops mental maps for memory storage.

The limbic part of the brain, described by Peters as the 'Chimp', is where the brain creates emotional responses. Its original function was to ensure the creation and survival of the next generation, either by responding to threats or driving the urge to procreate.

Whatever its use in evolution, scientists now believe it to be a powerful emotional machine which can either be your best friend or your worst enemy. Indeed, at its worst, this emotional centre can completely override your logical, human brain.

The final part of the brain – the parietal area - Peters refers to as the computer. This part contains storage areas and is where you'll find the automatic functioning machinery of the brain. It also stores information from both the Human and Chimp parts of the brain, so is a reference point for both logical thinking and emotion.

Peters has focused much of his work on the interaction between the two separate parts of the brain –the Human and the Chimp. These two parts are frequently in a state of battle, with the Human brain aiming to do nothing more than manage the Chimp. Controlling the Chimp is out of the question.

The battles, as Peters describes, are centred in four areas. These are:

- Ways of thinking
- Agendas
- Modes of operating
- Personalities

Exploring these in more detail helps explain how these battles impact your emotions, your behaviours and essential tasks such as decision-making.

WAYS OF THINKING

Peters describes this as how you interpret information you receive throughout the day.

The Human brain searches for facts to establish the truth and aims to use logical thought to form a plan as a response to what's happening around you.

In contrast, the Chimp relies on feelings and impressions to make sense of information. It generates emotional thinking and fills information gaps with beliefs and assumptions, rather than logic.

The great part of the Chimp is that it enables you to experience the 'gut feel' or instinctive hit we all recognise. Unfortunately, it's likely this hit gets obscured by the other emotional thoughts swirling around in the Chimp.

So, how does this look in real life?

In one of my workshops, I ask people how they start each day. Typically, participants describe repeated situations. The first thing they do is switch on the phone or laptop, start dealing with emails and get a sense of what's likely to come up during the day.

Let's look at one potential situation...

If, before you get into the office, you read a few emails that tell you three of your five staff are absent with sickness that day, you'll have major concerns about how work is going to be covered. In Peters' model, there are two potential interpretations occurring here.

The Chimp - as the most powerful - will take hold of this staffing information and gain control of your thoughts and feelings. It's likely to assign a range of feelings to this situation ranging from panic; overwhelm; feeling out of control; disbelief this is happening to you; anger at the employees for letting you down (again!), to triggering a long-held belief you're always singled out as the unlucky one.

As you can see, this type of emotional thinking is random, inconsistent and unpredictable. What's worse is there tends to be a self-perpetuating effect, where each feeling creates another more emotive thought, which in turn creates another impactful feeling, and so on.

In the end, as you may have experienced, the Chimp can create horrendous, catastrophic feelings which lead to powerful physical sensations. Your stomach churns, you feel the tight gripping tension headache, your pulse races and you feel paralysed. It can get to the point where the pain of just reading the email creates an inability to see a way forward.

It's typical of the Chimp part of the brain to create insecure thoughts. It constantly looks for danger (remember, it was created to ensure survival), so the thoughts it generates are usually paranoid, wary and mistrusting in nature.

Most importantly, the Chimp manages to cloud the realisation these feelings would come and go naturally, if left alone. Instead, the Chimp sees them as fact, in black and white with no shades of grey.

Getting gripped like this may happen all too often and certainly reflects the belief held by many, that all this bad stuff happening to us is outside our control and inevitable. The reality is so different.

To balance this understanding of the Chimp ways of thinking, you really need to look at what's happening with the Human brain. In reading the same email, with the same situation unfolding, the Human brain takes a different route.

It aims to remain calm, to understand the situation clearly and act rationally, based on fact. The Human brain will create opinion from fact and as such will not create a personal view of what's happening. This will lead to greater flexibility if the view is proven wrong and needs to change.

In our example, the Human brain will be trying to establish the facts about what the day will be like:

- How much really needs to be done today?
- Who else might be available to take on some of the work temporarily?
- What needs to be said to certain customers to manage their expectations?

Now remember, the Human brain also has to try to manage the emotions and thinking generated by the Chimp. It will try to override the Chimp's inconsistencies and step over feelings-driven behaviours.

Both the Human brain and the Chimp struggle in one shared area, they can both get distressed when the 'truth' as they see it cannot be established – either through facts or through feelings.

Once again, this is a great point to see where these minds look for the 'truth'.

The Chimp operates from the place of emotional thinking, based on its perception of the truth or projections of what might be the truth. This is unlike the Human brain, which searches for facts and logic to establish the truth.

You can see how easy it is to get mixed up with both of these inputs.

Whilst the Chimp works from feelings and emotional thinking, it does not realise these feeling pass or change very quickly and as such are an unreliable guide on which to base actions or behaviours.

In terms of decision-making, the Chimp is likely to form an opinion or make a decision quickly, without factual information, then seek information afterwards, to back up its stance.

Of course, the drive to prove it's right and protect its well-being, may mean having to manipulate facts for its own purpose. Added to this, the Chimp sees everything in only two dimensions – black and white – and cannot deal with ambiguity in the world today. This narrow perspective makes it more likely for Chimp-based thinking to come across as judgemental and removes its ability to scan for possible solutions.

The natural paranoia in the Chimp will also affect its judgement and decisions. It will do all it can to defend its stance and see any alternatives as a threat to be removed or dealt with defensively. Linked to this is the Chimp's defence system against danger; it causes interpretations which lead to a string of catastrophic future-based thinking.

For example, if there's a rumour at work that redundancies are a possibility, the Chimp will be at a high state of vigilance, watching for any signs this might be on the way for you. When it thinks it sees different behaviour in your boss and you're asked to attend an unexpected meeting with him, you can imagine what thoughts the Chimp creates.

Having a meeting with the boss, which should be a simple, everyday part of working life, suddenly leads to a stream of emotional thinking, based on the Chimp's fear of loss and its belief it needs to act to protect you. If the Chimp is allowed to take over, you'll notice a stream of thoughts which seem to map out the most dire consequences of that meeting – you're being made redundant; you'll be penniless; you'll not get another job; your wife will leave you; you'll lose the house; the children will disown you; you'll end up on the street homeless and penniless etc.....

Sound familiar?

I bet you've been down this route more than once and scarily enough it can be so powerful, you can almost believe it's real.

Set against this is the complete opposite ways of thinking created by the Human brain.

Remember, it bases its thinking and creation of reality on facts and finding the truth. In this, the human brain tries to find evidence before creating an opinion or acting. When it decides to create an action, it is based on rational thought processes, which are more consistent and structured than those of the Chimp. The Human brain is more open to other opinions and more able to accept that it might be wrong and change accordingly. The Human brain uses all of these methods in decision-making, basing decisions on logical thinking, rather than the more chaotic emotional thinking of the Chimp.

The Human brain will prepare for a meeting with the boss by collecting and assimilating facts. It goes in with an open mind, being prepared to hear what is said and, then, draw conclusions.

It will aim to listen with logic and act with objectivity (once it has managed the emotional impact of the Chimp, of course).

AGENDAS

The Human and the Chimp brains work to different agendas with regards their purpose. The Chimp exists to ensure survival and continued existence of the individual and species; the Human brain is focused on development, personal achievement and enabling us to fulfil our purpose in life.

You can see how these agendas bring conflict between the two brains.

The Chimp's two primary drives of procreation and survival are described more fully by Peters when he talks about the Chimp's Jungle Centre (see Modes of Operating, below).

The Human brain has drives associated with self-fulfilment and purpose, alongside creating and maintaining society.

I see the clash created by these conflicting agendas by how people behave in business. If an individual has a Human brain agenda for personal success and fulfilment, the Chimp can pick it up and use its 'jungle' ways of operating to ensure success.

It happens when you see someone who may start his career in business as an ethical, highly community focused person, but adopts more aggressive, bullying and politically manipulative behaviours. These behaviours derive from the drives and emotions of the Chimp allowed to run wild.

MODES OF OPERATING

The Chimp operates by following the laws of the jungle. These are more instinctive, crudely developed and almost prehistoric in nature but are enormously powerful.

Contrast this with the Human brain which operates from a place of strong conscience, morality and ethics.

The Chimp's 'Jungle Centre' contains the beliefs and behaviours the Chimp knows work well for ensuring survival. It has several distinct operational features, including:

> **Instincts**

These are built-in responses or reactions, present from birth, and often triggered by some kind of stimuli. You'll be aware of the common instincts of flight, fright or freeze, which are automatic responses to danger designed to protect you. In a situation perceived to be 'dangerous', the Chimp offers these instincts to the Human as a course of action. Any one of these reactions evokes a strong emotion, which encourages you to act quickly. Typically, the Human brain will chose flight (run away) or freeze (avoid conflict).

Here's an example to help you see how instinct shows up in our everyday lives:

Imagine you've just walked into a room full of strangers. You'll notice an instant reaction –you can either 'fight' (stand your ground and establish your presence), 'freeze' (try not to be noticed and find a quiet corner to stand in) or 'flight' (aim to leave immediately). Your Chimp will feel under threat and your Human brain will try to manage the situation by taking control and rationalising the situation, drawing on past experiences, using logic and a calm mind.

If however, you don't choose any one of the fight, freeze or flight options, the experience of the reaction intensifies. More adrenalin is produced and more negative thoughts are generated, as the Chimp enters a heightened anxious state. It will try to push you into making a decision, as the threat grows. The Human brain will continue to calm and reassure, even in the face of increasingly catastrophic thoughts. You can feel the struggle.

> **Drives**

Your drives are what compel you to do things every day, to fulfil your real or perceived needs. The Chimp has powerful drives to ensure the continuation of the species. These are compelling and difficult to resist.

For example, there is a strong eating drive in all of us. We are compelled to eat and this drive when not managed takes us from the desire to eat one doughnut to the compunction to gorge on as many as possible. The Human brain tries to counter this drive with a fact: one doughnut is enough. And so another struggle begins. All drives are supported and reinforced by strong reward pathways in the brain, where chemicals and positive thoughts are generated, encouraging repeat behaviour.

You can see why managing eating and weight loss is often referred to as a 'battle' because, in the mind, it is precisely what is being played out.

> **Personalities**

The Human brain and the Chimp clearly display different personality traits. The Human brain is more logical, calm and aims to find evidence before coming to judgements or decisions. The Human brain operates from values and qualities it holds as its part in humanity. These qualities include:

- Honesty
- Compassion
- Having a conscience
- Self-control
- Following laws or rules
- Having a sense of purpose
- Creating achievements and satisfaction

These qualities are very different from the drives and traits displayed by the Chimp as part of its 'Jungle Centre'.

There's an added complication in these two competing personality types. The Chimp can display different traits, as there are male and female Chimp variations. These characteristics are influenced by hormones and are found in male and females in varying degrees. This takes competing personalities from two-dimensional to multi-dimensional.

Even in this brief overview of how the brain is structured, the physiology behind the way you think shows how thoughts are not as straightforward as they seem. Thoughts and emotions are closely tied to the emotional centre of the brain. You can see how the idea you need to manage thoughts has evolved. Knowing the conscious Human brain has this management role, creates a belief that thoughts aligned with emotion need to be controlled, otherwise the whole thought-emotion cycle will get out of control.

MANAGING THINKING

There's a scientific way to look at how our brain works to help us manage our thinking.

David Rock[2] who has written many books on leadership development, has recently worked with neuroscientists to determine what happens inside the brain and how it can so easily reach its biological limits every day. His work aims to shed light on how and why we feel overwhelmed by the amount of processing and thinking we demand of our conscious-thinking part of the brain.

Neuroscientists continue to research how this part of the brain can be better supported simply by managing the amount of energy used to process different types of information.

Neuroscientists distinguish between the brain as a functioning organ in the body and the mind, which they describe as a regulator of the brain. They believe if you know how your brain works, you can use your mind to change habits to enable it to work more efficiently.

They have discovered the pre-frontal cortex part of your brain is crucial in processing information, making decisions, creating new thoughts and inhibiting or controlling impulses. This sounds a lot like the Human mind described by Peters.

The main issue with the pre-frontal cortex (or thinking part of the brain) is its major capacity limitations, which impact its function over time. It only makes up four percent of the total volume of the brain and so easily becomes overwhelmed if the information load is too great or the processing too complex.

When neuroscientists talk about processing information, it's not one simple, linear task. There are up to five processes going on within one overall activity. To process a single piece of information, the brain needs to do any one of or all of the following:

1. Recall - bringing past information from memory back into current thinking as a reference source.

2. Memorising – creating a mental map of a piece of information, so it can be held in memory and pulled out again if needed e.g. remembering a face when you meet someone for the first time.

3. Inhibiting - this is a process of trying to retain focus and not allowing too many competing facts or pieces of information to fill the processing space in the brain at any one time. This function also involves controlling emotional thoughts

4. Deciding – in this process, the brain tries to support decision-making through comparing one piece of information with other pieces of information.

5. Understanding – how to process and make sense of a new idea. This will involve delving into memory to access mental maps of part or finding new facts to make sense of what's happening now.

On top of these processes, there's another factor impacting the effective functioning of the brain – the amount of energy used in processing. Processing is a conscious mental activity, using up vast quantities of energy, which is not infinitely available to the brain.

If you've ever experienced the two o'clock 'fog', this is a sign your brain processing battery is running out of energy. It can be topped up by fuelling your body with food or sweet drinks, but it will never be as efficient as at the start of the day.

To counter this, we are able to operate with some automatic processes, created through repetition of certain activities.

For example, when you realise you no longer notice the activity of driving your car, you know you've moved it into a place where little mental attention is required. Through repetition, driving has become a largely automatic activity.

However, if you then drove into in an unfamiliar area – where you had no idea of the turns to be made – suddenly you'd become very aware of your driving activity. You move the whole operation into conscious thought to process new or unknown information effectively.

There are a few ways you can manage the limitations of your pre-frontal cortex and the subsequent impact it has on your thinking power.

Neuroscientists recommend you aim to reduce the load on the pre-frontal cortex by writing down as much as you can. You can using visual images to make new concepts easier to retain, prioritise thinking and creatively solve problems at the beginning of the day or following a rest.

Mixing up the type of tasks you do in the day will also help lighten the processing load and make your brain work more efficiently.

MINIMISING DISTRACTIONS

Another way of reducing the amount of brain processing overload and its impact on your thinking capacity is to minimise distractions.

We're more aware than ever of the impact of external distraction on our lives through the rise of 24-7, 'always on' technology.

We are encouraged to turn off our mobile phones and reset our email notifications, to enable us to minimise interruptions and the processing impact these have on our brain.

External distractions not only affect us in the moment; their effect results in the need for us to continually re-focus and this takes a lot of mental energy. Given we need mental energy to support the five core processes of the conscious thinking part of the brain, reducing distractions is an essential step in improving our thinking capacity.

Internal distractions are harder to control. You know how your mind becomes filled with random and strange thoughts at the oddest times? Your mind naturally likes to wander, largely due to the constant processing, reconfiguring and re-connecting taking place in the brain at all times. On average, you hold a thought for 10 seconds before it passes and your attention moves to another.

Rock compares managing these internal distractions as a rider (conscious will) trying to control the larger and uncontrollable 'elephant' which is the unconscious mind.

The need to control and manage comes up in other parts of this book. Which demonstrates how important these elements are perceived to be by development theorists and experts.

The need to understand brain physiology and how the mind works has moved from research into the personal and business world. You now need to grasp the concepts studied by neuroscientists, apply a range of techniques to improve how your brain works and win the battle between Human and Chimp brains.

Set this against the daily demands in business, it's clear how you are facing a challenge. How to 'do' all this, know as much as you can and change how you operate to manage your processing powers.

I've always found it interesting to understand the physiology behind actions and behaviours and I know how enticing it can be to believe this knowledge will help manage the stress and overwhelm of everyday life. In my experience, putting any of this into practice is more difficult than understanding the concepts.

That's where meltdown begins.

AN ALTERNATIVE APPROACH TO... HOW YOUR MIND WORKS

The work carried out by neuroscientists and thought leaders such as Steven Peters take us a long way down the road of understanding how our brain works. Whatever the model, there is agreement that in our evolution we first developed a highly responsive limbic (emotional) system, designed to invoke measures to protect ourselves and ensure continuation of the species. It obviously served us well at the time.

However, our continued evolution as 'thinking beings' has led to a system conflict. In it, the emotional centre creates a strong impact on our more reasoned, controlled, conscious-thinking system.

In addition to managing the emotional centre, our conscious

thought system is now facing increased demands through the sheer volume of information it processes daily.

No wonder we are constantly looking for ways to re-balance and bring a sense of equilibrium to our mind and our brain. As a result, we are offered suggestions on how to 'manage our thinking'. These range from managing our information load through to developing awareness of the Chimp's impact.

In my view, whilst these methods of management have some limited success, it's time for a paradigm shift. These ideas are created by the thinking and beliefs of others. Whilst they add to your knowledge and understanding, that's not enough to give you a permanent shift in how you operate. The sheer number of ways to 'manage your thinking', indicates none of them hold the real solution. The shift in paradigm will move you away from following these methods, to the realisation you can let go and naturally allow your own ways of dealing with thoughts and emotions to emerge.

In life and in business, it's time to move away from developing methods to control or manage thinking and move towards a different view of what's available in the realms of thought.

To illustrate this, let's look at how you might use your thinking to achieve a certain target.

Traditional paradigms focus on how you can control thoughts. To achieve a target, you begin with the thoughts needed to set a target and measures. Then, you create an action plan, detailing the steps needed to achieve the goal. Alongside this, you're encouraged to develop additional techniques, designed to calm the emotional centre to minimise feelings of fear and anxiety activated in the limbic system.

Each step in this process comes from thoughts, generated from your personal mind (Human mind and Chimp, combined). You draw on past experiences and mental maps, providing you with everything you need to create and achieve the goal in mind.

These past experiences enable your brain to offer many possible success routes to achieve the outcome you're looking for. Less helpfully, it also offers many examples of where failure has occurred, as a warning and an attempt at self-protection.

If all of this is available why, then, is it so difficult to achieve a target you set yourself?

If you know what to do and how to do it, what goes wrong?

When you really stop and notice, you'll start to experience the emotions and behaviours associated with each of these personal thoughts. Each time you have this experience, these thoughts and emotions seem absolutely real to you.

If you habitually failed to reach a target, chances are, the thoughts and emotions you experience will reinforce everything that went wrong in the past. After all, the emotional centre in your brain is connected to your conscious mind and is always there to warn you, protect you and keep you from the 'danger of failure'.

If you allow these old thought patterns to dominate, you find yourself in an old pattern of thinking and behaving. This will, no doubt, take you right back to the familiar place of not quite succeeding.

How can you trust yourself if this is what's going on?

All it takes is a shift in what you understand about your thoughts. This is the paradigm shift.

Instead of generating and following each of these personal thoughts and believing the scenarios they create are real, you can start to see them for what they are – simply illusions which appear real to you.

When you know each thought will be replaced by another, then another and another, you can let those thoughts simply enter your mind then leave. This allows your mind to function with the time, space and energy, required to 'hear' your more instinctive, inner wisdom.

The difference with this paradigm is the understanding of where your thoughts come from. When you tune into your inner wisdom, rather than your personal thoughts, you automatically find the balance needed for better decisions, clearer thinking and less overwhelm.

You're able to trust wholeheartedly in these new thoughts, as they come from a place free from past experiences and emotions. They have been created from a more stable place, free from 'historical thought'.

Interestingly, thoughts created through your inner wisdom may suggest the target or goal you originally believed you needed to follow, was taking you to the wrong outcome. The inner wisdom may cause you to shift focus to a new set of intentions, rather than the rigidity of a preconceived set of goals. The bottom line is, when you let go of your personal thinking, you create more space for the natural re-balancing of your system and new thinking to emerge.

You may continue to follow a particular goal-setting route, or you may shift to something completely different. The crux is, your innate wisdom will show you the path as it opens up, as long as you are tuned in enough to notice.

What does this mean in your business?

Quite simply, it means this. When you put less effort into fixing or controlling your thoughts or those of your people, you will find a lot more head space. In this, you'll be able to tune into instinctive, natural solutions. The push and effort you believe is required to work through issues, reduces and the pressure comes off.

Instead of management and control, encourage your employees to 'let go'. Suspend any activity designed to 'fix' their thoughts and trust the way forward will open up before them.

Tune in to hearing your own wisdom and trust your people's inner wisdom and stop working so hard to fix problems (which aren't actually real!)

Once you've shifted to this way of operating, you can create all the steps and plans needed, but from a different place. It is a place more aligned to what will naturally work and requires a lot less effort.

CHAPTER THREE:
THE POWER OF TRUST

To begin to understand yourself, experience demonstrates the best place to start is trust.

In my work with individuals and teams, the foundation of good relationships, both with others and within yourself, is trust. If this is absent, it's really difficult to form any kind of effective, sustainable relationship.

Trust is a word or sentiment, used often and yet not to its real intent. We express it as a measure of reality, but whose reality does it measure?

To me, trust is a multi-faceted emotion, which expresses how we feel about ourselves and our ability to deliver. It also expresses how much others feel able to rely on us to deliver for them. It is a feelings-based cornerstone of how we view ourselves and how others perceive us.

Ask yourself this:

- How much do you trust your thinking?
- How do you trust your instincts?

- Are you able to trust others when they are out to deceive and hide things from you?
- How are you trustworthy when you are wearing many masks designed to hide who you are and how you are feeling?

I'll explore what we mean by trust and where it shows up in our lives, starting with self-trust and self-belief and then looking at gaining trust from others. Trust will also re-emerge later in the book, when we look at relationships between each other.

SELF-TRUST

A number of years ago, I read a book by Stephen M.R.Covey[3] (son of the Stephen Covey, author of 7 Habits of Highly Effective People [4]) and it had a profound impact on me at the time. It was called The Speed of Trust.

At the time it was written (some seven years ago) it felt pertinent, but now it's incredible how the notion of trust has become a core factor in the success or failure of people and businesses. You just need to look at the banking sector to see the ripples of broken trust spreading far beyond the organisations.

Taking the Libor scandal, as an example. How do you trust banks and their leaders when their actions in fixing borrowing rates between banks were hidden and denied, until they were forced to acknowledge the true extent of the corruption only when investigated? Looking further back to the economic collapse of 2008, did you trust the investment decisions made by banks? We believed they would result in growth and return on investment, rather than huge risk-taking and financial collapse.

WHAT THE THEORIES SAY

Many psychologists believe finding trust is an important stage in early human development.

If a child successfully experiences trust he or she will ultimately develop into a positive, optimistic individual. If, however, trust is not found or lost in the early years, the child will feel pessimistic, insecure and mistrusting of others.

Other psychologists see trust as a personality trait. If you are pre-disposed to be trusting, you will find it easier to form relationships and build positive outcomes.

I'm not going to explore every theory or model of trust. Instead, I will focus on just one part, the trust we have in ourselves to do what we set out to do.

When looking at trust, Covey describes it as something to be grown and nurtured, rather than something which does or doesn't exist.

He views the creation of trust as a two-part process: the first part where you give trust – to yourself and others – and the second part where you want others to trust you – your trustworthiness.

He describes this process as the beginning of good change, within each individual. He labels his first 'wave of trust' as self-trust. He defines this as how much confidence you have in yourself to be and do all that you set out to.

Covey then encourages you to ask the following questions to fully gauge where your own level of self-trust lies:

- How confident are you that you can set and, more importantly, achieve goals?
- Do you believe you can keep to commitments?
- If you make these public, can you be confident you can walk the talk?

In basic terms trust is all about doing what is expected of you, whether its expectations set from within yourself or by others.

It's interesting, trust, as described by Covey is so closely linked with goal-setting. Knowing how tough it can be to set and achieve goals, it's easy to see how self-trust can be an elusive state to attain.

To be confident in walking the talk, Covey says you need to have four core elements. Two of these are character-based:

- Integrity – being honest and congruent with who you really are. In other words, not lying and being authentic.
- Positive intent – not trying to deceive or protect others.

Making sure you don't hold hidden motives or have another hidden agenda running the show.

The other two elements are competence-based:

- Capabilities or credentials – do you actually have the knowledge, skills and expertise you profess to have?
- Results – do you really have the track record you claim to have, so you can demonstrate a range of results in different situations? Do you and others around you, believe you will continue to do demonstrate those results?

It might seem that if you have these elements in place, you're all sorted on the trust front. If any are missing perhaps you believe you can 'borrow' trust or create it for yourself by virtue of your role or position.

But, in reality, an external label of a role title won't have you really believe in yourself and so create self-trust.

Instead, you're more likely to be using up a lot of energy every day thinking about how you're OK, how you will achieve the results you say you can demonstrate (no matter how many times you've failed to in the past) and believing you're good enough to be trusted by virtue of the image you present to the world.

Worst of all, you might be using up a lot of emotional energy finding ways to protect yourself from being found out. Ultimately, failing to take the time to re-discover or create self-trust will cost you more in the long term, so it's worthwhile doing all you can to prevent the loss of this trust over the years.

EROSION OF SELF-TRUST

If self-trust is about delivering what you commit to, this takes us to the area of goal setting and achievement. Every day in business I hear people talking about the need to set clear goals, create definite plans and get on and achieve them.

It's what drives change programmes and plans in so many businesses. It feels like the endless diet and exercise cycle, where new goals and resolutions are made daily. And yet, if it were this simple, you wouldn't constantly be in a cycle of setting and re-setting goals would you?

On a personal level, how often have you made goals – even shared them with others – and yet repeatedly failed to achieve them? Goal-setting and implementation is seen as the path to success by so many.

We so often hear: make your goals stretching; get out of your comfort zone; push a little harder to achieve more...and yet so many of us never quite make the grade and succeed in achieving what we're striving for.

We end up in a miserable cycle of setting goals, taking some action, then finding something de-rails us from reaching the end point.

This goal-setting failure dichotomy is one I hear repeated in so many parts of people's lives and have experienced myself. Failing to achieve goals sets you on the road to meltdown, where you experience stress, overwhelm and loss of self-belief.

With my clients, we focus on what outcomes they want to achieve through their work with me.

Often they make a statement about a specific goal, something they really want to change, which has proved elusive over past attempts. I'm usually curious about these public statements of a goal. I will always try to help the client be really clear about why achieving the goal is important and what they believe will change as a result.

It's obvious at this stage the client is really committed to making change happen, with statements like "it's going to work this time" and "I'm really going to push myself". What transpires is often very different.

What really interests me is the tracking of progress against a goal. Quite often when I check in with my client, they have failed to make the progress they had hoped or 'slipped off the wagon'. There's a sense of overwhelm when they feel the scale of the task and the fear once again they may not achieve the goal.

At this point, I stop them and explore the cycle of repeated goal-setting, where they are energised by the buzz of commitment to something transformational, but acutely feel the defeat when the outcome fails to materialise.

In these clients there's a strong sense of more than one process at work. It's almost as if they have a push-pull energy; as they get closer to achieving their goal, something else steps in to pull them away.

We can all get into the cycle of repeatedly setting goals, feeling the buzz of commitment but time and time again failing to see it through. There is a great deal of rationalising, justifying and logical thinking feeding this process and yet there's a lot of feeling there too.

You really feel the excitement of what's possible, the camaraderie, and the sense of how life could be different if success is achieved. There's also a lot of feeling when success seems to slip away: disappointment and frustration, moving on to self-loathing, feelings of failure and, perhaps, even despair. The risk of meltdown becomes real, as the feelings move from disappointment to catastrophe.

The problem is, as Covey points out, if we can't trust our own commitments and our ability to deliver results, we erode our sense of self-trust and our confidence in our ability to deliver. When you move this from an individual experience into a business context, you can see how business performance can actually fall when challenging goals are set.

I see the same process and resulting frustration happen within whole businesses when there is a goal to make change happen in some area.

As a people change manager, drafted in to help system or process-based change programmes work, I see business leaders make public statements about what will change, how great it will be and how beneficial it will be for everyone.

Unfortunately, often the process of change is focused on changing technical or process aspects, rather than focusing on people and how change affects them.

This is an important distinction, as people change typically takes an adaptive approach. This is a cyclical process of 'learn – action – development' designed to enable people to engage with change beyond the rational level. As we are all complex human systems there's a lot more to achieving a goal or making a change than taking logical steps and following a process.

In my experience, a lot of thinking and emotion needs to be addressed first, both individually and as a team.

APPROACHES TO CHANGE IN BUSINESS

The issue facing any business leader focused on change is the collective power of thought and habitual thought. If you are a leader trying to change something in your business, you'll probably be guided through methodical approaches – such as Kotter's[5] 8 steps or Lewin's[6] change model. These give guidance on the process to follow when taking people with you on the change journey.

I recently worked with a leader who was delighted to find the book *From Hippos to Gazelles*[7] used fantastic metaphors and imagery based on tribal ways of living. These were cleverly applied to corporate change needs.

For him, this way of telling the story gave him a clear framework to follow. He believed that if he followed each step as outlined, he would be successful at creating a new globally-dispersed function with an aligned team and seamless processes.

All these models provide great sources of information and processes which aim to bring success, if, of course, all steps are followed and with the same level of skill as the author and the consultants used.

Approaches like Kotter's 8 step change process only work to a limited degree, as people following the process often fail to look deeper into the 'being' side of change. By this I mean making the connection with the people involved and looking deeper than their apparent needs, obstacles and behaviours.

In these processes, there is a high degree of judgement that the old ways are wrong, that individual concerns are damaging and that 'winning' is the only way. Often change processes are designed to bring about coercion or enforcement of change, as the outcome being 'the right thing to do'.

Using these models in this way, is based on particular beliefs and thoughts created by the models' authors. The aim being to change thoughts, feelings and behaviours in others through various external techniques applied to each person involved. Unfortunately, this does nothing, as in reality each person cannot be made to feel or think a certain way.

What seems an obvious and valuable outcome of change in one person, may not be the same for someone else. After all, we are totally unique in the thoughts and experiences we have.

Equally, we can see how riddled with assumptions and inaccuracies the area of trust and self-trust can be. Fundamentally, the only real control we have over our ability to achieve sits within each of us, not within a process or theory on how to manage or achieve what we set out to.

What will break the erosion cycle?

To maintain a sense of self-trust, be it with setting and achieving your own goals or by publicly leading change, the models say there are a few steps to be followed.

Looking at the broader change management and leadership models of Kotter et al and you'll see clearly the need to follow a formula or tried-and-tested steps.

As you become more skilled and experienced, you'll feel freer to address some of the trickier behavioural issues which crop up when people around you are going through change. Bringing adaptive change alongside technical change is not somewhere everyone is prepared to go, but the models reinforce that all parts of change need to be covered.

When looking at self-trust from an individual place, the focus on management and personal development will be on achieving the goals in the best way possible. However, if it was as easy as this, we'd not need coaches, dieting clubs, personal trainers and management consultants etc. to break the cycle of repeated failure.

We need to look at some other processes going on.

To understand ourselves more fully, it seems right to go deeper, step away from the well-documented process of goal-setting and discover what might be happening underneath, as a way to break out of the cycle of defeat and re-build trust.

There's been some interesting work carried out by Kegan and Lahey[8] who researched this issue, both in individuals and in organisations. They called the phenomenon 'Immunity to Change'.

They questioned what was going on when, on the surface, people were very committed to their goals and made changes required to achieve them ... yet succumbed to self-sabotage over and over. As a result of their research, they developed a useful process for shedding light on why we get into the goal-setting–failure cycle and developed a way to escape from it.

Crucially, it highlights how knowing yourself better helps unblock this part of your life. If you try to make changes in your life, gaining clarity on hidden beliefs or commitments can remove obstacles you didn't even know were there.

Here's an overview of the process Kegan and Lahey created:

Uncovering your immunity to change

The first step in understanding is to identify a really important or urgent compelling goal to change something in your life.

The next step is to make a list of all the things you're doing to support achieving this goal and anything you're doing which doesn't support achieving the goal.

If, for, example, your goal is to exercise more to get fit, you may start increasing the amount of time you spend exercising and aim to go to the gym every day after work.

The next crucial step is to create a worry list. These are all the things you think might happen if you do all the things in support of achieving your goal.

To continue with the fitness example, you might add to your worry list the fear that leaving work to exercise might mean you don't get all your work done. You can take it further to uncover what that means for you:

"Leaving work to exercise means I'll be the first to leave, it might look as though I'm not committed to my job, where others are staying behind. I might therefore be overlooked when the next promotion opportunity comes up, my career therefore will be over and I will never succeed in work."

When you uncover these hidden beliefs, you can see an interesting picture emerge. There's a pull between achieving the stated goal and all the hidden things you're equally committed to. This awareness is interesting, but to really gain clarity about why you aren't achieving your goal, you need to go deeper.

There are hidden beliefs which lead to behaviours, which in turn take you away from achieving your goal. These seem to be there for a reason as they serve a hidden purpose. The purpose may be to protect you from something you believe will happen, or drive you towards a different outcome which, at some level, feels preferential to the external goal you've stated.

This is why it's important for you to uncover the major assumptions you're making. Until you do, your motivations will cause you to feel like you're pulling in a different direction. It may be a blind spot you have or a belief keeping your behaviours on different tracks. Getting your beliefs and behaviours together is how you achieve what you set out to do.

The key to uncovering the blind spot is to go back to your worry list and all the hidden commitments you've uncovered and ask yourself – "What's true about that?" for each of them.

Back to our example. You've created an assumption or belief that success at work is wrapped up in being seen to be present, being there more than others and so needing to minimise your life outside work.

These thoughts might be based on previous experiences or beliefs, or even just constructed out of what you perceive has happened to others.

Does staying at work, working longer hours than everyone else and being seen to be present and minimising time outside work really make you more likely to be successful and get promoted at work?

When you see it like this, you're unlikely to agree "yes" to all your hidden assumptions.

Once this belief or pattern of thought is exposed, you'll find it much easier to change the behaviours to those which give you the outcome you really want.

When you get the outcome, you'll start building more trust in your own ability to deliver and be consistent - your self-trust.

What's interesting in the process Kegan and Lahey created is how much it revolves around your thought patterns, past experiences and current behaviours. It steers you on a route to manage these thoughts, to bring experiences to the fore and, by following all the steps, create a new set of behaviours.

EROSION OF TRUSTWORTHINESS

It's easy to erode trust and watch it slip away. Being trustworthy or wanting others to trust you can only develop when self-trust is in place.

As I've mentioned, there are many recent examples where business leaders have taken part in some major actions, such as the Enron collapse and the Libor scandal, which destroy trust in them or their business. My sense is, they believed their role titles and positions of power would generate trust and absolve them from the need to be trustworthy.

Equally, every time you do or say something an employee, colleague or customer might perceive as a lie, it erodes their trust in you and your trustworthiness. Even something as simple as pretending to be in a meeting, when you're not, loses a little bit of trust in you.

We underestimate the degree to which our actions create reactions in others. When I see these behaviours, I hear a lot of self-justification and explanation, which creates a seemingly robust reason why we fail to deliver on an agreement or deceive others. Later in the book, we'll take a closer look at trust in relationships. Being perceived as trustworthy is an essential factor in sustaining positive relationships and cannot be easily repaired.

Losing a little trustworthiness may seem small in the moment, but done continually it will eventually result in a big deficit, which you'll struggle to redeem when you most need it in the future.

As a leader, failing to follow through on your public commitments leads to a huge loss of trust through loss of credibility and loss of belief in your results.

In reality, the only way to retrieve and re-build is through honesty and authenticity. This occurs through being able to show your vulnerability, your ability to fail and your willingness to re-position the outcome.

AN ALTERNATIVE APPROACH TO.... TRUST

In all these models, there's a similar theme, where we are being 'helped' into being a better person through research and theory.

What would happen if we took all these away?

How would we know what to do when working with others?

How would we achieve what we set out to do?

How would we change?

Where would we be?

We would be in a place without 'how to'... or 'ought to'... or 'need to'.

We would be in place without ego.

People talk about ego, yet I wonder if how many people stop to consider what it really means. It's something often described in derogatory terms, as if it is something everyone else has and you don't.

We all have an ego – something which gives us an image of our own self-importance. It purports to serve us by protecting us, by ensuring we act in the right way and keeps us secure by knowing our place in the world.

If you look around at nature, you don't see ego. You'll not see an oak tree casting its shadow wider and deeper than other trees, just because it can. Instead, you'll see nature creating balance where the needs of all the trees and creatures around them are met and working in synergy.

Given then we are part of nature, you can't help but wonder where our natural balance has gone.

What has us jostle for space, complain when others have what we don't, and feel embattled with others around us?

It's ego which creates this sense. The ego creates in us the fear we will be over-run, taken over, even destroyed by others. It creates thoughts telling us this is true and in response we feel fear, frustration, anxiety, stress and depression.

You can see in this description how the Chimp brain is at work to create these ego-based thoughts, behaviours and emotions.

These thoughts are focused on the external world around us, telling us what should or shouldn't be done to head off problems and clear a better path.

Ego exists within us and manifests through our thoughts.

You know when it's around; our thoughts are coloured by a sense of catastrophe, fear and impending doom. It shows up under the guise of thinking about being in control, managing things or people in our environment. Many development models and processes aim to change who we are and the impact of our ego.

At times when you've been immune to change and you understand the thoughts which blocking you from making changes, where does it leave you in the long run?

In all likelihood, it's created more thoughts about how stupid you were to not see the competing commitments, the limiting beliefs and the assumptions you believed were true. You might even feel frustrated because you can see how you never achieved your goals and how you allowed all the false assumptions to get in the way.

You see, an alternative to all these theories is a simple one. Take away the ego, notice the cascade of analysing, self-deprecating thoughts and aim to generate fewer personal thoughts, judgements and analysis.

What you're left with is the space to 'be'.

In this space, you'll notice something remarkable. All the answers, knowledge and understanding you need is already there for you to call on. You don't need protecting from the outside world because you are naturally creative, capable and complete. Just as you are.

This understanding is muffled by the noise of self-doubt and the ramblings of ego-based thoughts which created a reality which isn't, in fact, real at all.

For an alternative view of how to understand ourselves, consider the premise it is far less important to focus on what we think. Instead, imagine looking at the principle that it is our thinking which creates our unique experience in life...or the fact 'that' we think.

To be aware we are the thinker puts us in the driver's seat. We choose the life we create and the outcomes we achieve simply through the 'fact' of knowing we are the thinker.

What if there's a different way to understand and develop self-trust?

If we go back to the example of the fitness goal. Often when people aspire to make changes in their lives, the drive or perceived need comes from a belief that when change arrives, everything will be better.

Have you ever heard the reasoning people often use:

"I'll be happy when..." or "I'll be successful when..."?

In this way of thinking, an individual places their happiness or success in the hands of an outside event. Even if we follow Kegan and Lahey's lead, we believe we'll be successful in breaking our 'immunity to change' when we correct all the components getting in the way.

This way of thinking transforms us into helpless beings which are buffeted by the outside world. If this was the case, when would we ever feel in control of our own outcomes, feelings and behaviours? How could we ever avoid feelings of overwhelm, loss of focus and stress?

The alternative is to embrace the idea you are the only one who can create the outcome you want. Only you can create feelings of happiness and success, through your own thinking.

Our very powerful mind has a habit of creating the illusion success will be forthcoming once another event or outcome is achieved. What most people find, however, is this isn't the case.

Achieving a goal, when it happens, brings a momentary feeling of elation and self-congratulation – but does it automatically bring the answer to the happy life you aspire to? Does it solve the feelings of low self-esteem, lack of confidence or lack of belief your thoughts had you believe?

Equally, if you follow a leadership development model which says you'll be a great leader when you have developed all the right elements, will you really reach this state?

Take trust as an example. What Covey says about building and maintaining trust might be true, and as a model it reflects the thinking of its researchers and creators. However, in itself, Covey's book will never truly bring about lasting trust and trustworthiness in yourself or from others.

Why is this?

Fundamentally, the whole model misses some important truths about how we operate.

One of those truths is we create each and every thought and we experience each thought. What we don't do is experience the event or circumstance outside us; we only ever experience our thoughts about it.

To put it simply, we didn't experience a lack of trust when news about the Libor scandal or MP's expenses became public. We only experienced our thoughts about these events and these may have differed from day to day too.

This experience may have shown up through feelings of anger, outrage or behaviours such as writing letters to the press or your MP. Just as easily, some people may have created positive thoughts leading to a different experience, such as feelings of admiration or wondering how they too could "get away with something so clever".

In this way, to really develop and maintain trust, we need to look at our own thoughts and decide which ones are valid and meaningful and which need to be discarded.

What if all these thoughts are destructive?

I can understand the fear of complete social and moral breakdown at this point. We have a personal store of thoughts borne out of a collection of memories, experiences and beliefs we've gathered over our lifetime.

If we were only able to notice these thoughts, we might be in a bit of trouble. In a way, the development models created over the years aim to control and manage this possibility.

However, there is another truth which takes the origin of thought to a totally new level. It is this: you have access to an infinite source of wisdom which, when called upon, provides you with a whole different type of thought and therefore experience.

This wisdom creates the natural balance and flow which keeps you aligned with your purpose and your true self. When you access thoughts from this place, you are not constrained or dictated to by past fears or experiences; you only need to deal with the present and what feels intuitively right.

This is where the real power of an understanding of thought lies. It does not come from outside. It does not need to be managed or controlled. It only needs space to be 'heard'.

I encourage you to look at these perspectives as I do, as pointers to the power of thought.

Development models are created from thoughts of people who accessed their own wisdom in an attempt to change our thinking patterns just a little, to something more positive and creative.

All you need to do now is look at each of these models from a different place – from the understanding you alone create your thoughts, you alone experience these thoughts and you alone have access to infinite wisdom. From here, any model might help to inspire insight or application, but will never in themselves create the solutions you're looking for.

These models will change over time, as new thoughts and research are generated. But the simple truth that we create our thoughts, we become aware of these thoughts and experience them alongside the endless supply of wisdom will never change. It's a constant.

You really don't need these frameworks or theories in order to 'improve yourself'.

You are already as good and capable of being the leader you want to be or living the life you want to live.

Use these theories to open the door to how your thinking creates behaviours and feelings in you and others.

Use these theories and frameworks as guides to help enhance your thinking, taking you to feelings of empathy, compassion and openness to the people around you.

Use these theories to supplement your instinctive wisdom, not to create more 'doing'.

You will never have control over the events, circumstances or information around you but you will always have the ability to understand the nature of your thoughts, which in turn will allow you to change the nature of the world you are in.

This is as much as you need to do.

How does this affect our change goals?

Using this new perspective on the subject of achieving a goal, you can understand now you create all your thoughts associated with goal-setting. You can change the experience of trying to reach a goal, if not the outcome, through the thoughts you create.

I don't mean managing thoughts, trying to make them positive or trying to visualise different outcomes, which is what most models suggest. Look somewhere totally different to make a change.

By tuning out of logic, reasoning, and the how and why of your personal (ego-driven) thoughts, you tune into your instinct. You will find all you need right there to achieve your goal, if it is a goal that serves you well.

This is a big 'if'. I see many development models coming from the place where well-researched outcomes are the only ones which achieve the 'right' outcome.

But, have you ever considered some goals don't serve us?

Some goals take us further way from the place of balance and flow we all instinctively long for. If you focus on achieving something which takes us further away from our natural state, you'll find the energy and effort required is substantially greater than what is needed to take you closer to where you need to be.

In my experience, when a particular goal was never the answer in the first place, it derived from a hope that a set of more positive feelings would be created as a result.

Sometimes, even having such thoughts will create a shift. In the short term you'll experience positive feelings associated with taking action and finally gaining control. But, over time, these emotions will once again be clouded with repetitive thoughts of "I'm not good enough; I'll be better when..."

Once again, we're back to the place where all change lies in the hands of external events and processes. Just remember, this is a misunderstanding. When you see the misunderstanding, you will see how development theories are trying to create change from the outside in.

In doing so, they will have you running in circles, trying to make the change work and be sustained. Anyone would buckle under this pressure. It doesn't need to be this way, remember all change comes from within you, from accessing your deeper wisdom.

CHAPTER FOUR: AUTHENTICITY

Authentic is defined by the Oxford English dictionary as:

Of undisputed origin and not a copy; genuine.

Authenticity is described as:

The quality or condition of being authentic, trustworthy, or genuine.

Defining, identifying and measuring authenticity is an area of development which consumes vast quantities of research and analysis. It seems to be the hardest trait to pin down and define.

On closer inspection, you can see why. To discover if someone is being authentic, somehow development models have to differentiate what is genuine and not 'copied' in each person. I'm sure you know how hard it is to define what is genuine about yourself and what has been adopted as a result of socialisation with others.

Authenticity is seen as an important attribute in all managers and leaders, partly because of the trustworthiness it instils (as above) and partly because it signifies less impact from the ego. With this out of the way - many theories state – leaders can be more effective at leading others from a solid place of truth, rather than inconsistent half-truths.

So many leaders or managers believe once they've assumed a new role or title, they have to change who they are.

Are you one of those?

For some, I've seen this happen quickly as a result of the recruitment processes. Perhaps it's something to do with the nature of selection methods which require you to upsell your skills and experience.

The process of focusing on yourself, your achievements and the great things you've achieved creates a story. Each time in the telling, the story becomes a little more exaggerated, a little more embellished and, in the process, becomes adopted by your ego to become create an illusion of reality.

The downside is, the person soon loses sight of who they are. They believe every detail of their story and 'the hype' takes over. After all, the story seems to work, so why throw away something which seems to have success written all over it?

For others, they seem to take on the persona or veneer they've picked up through training, or watching their boss operate, or by copying the behaviours of someone they perceive to be successful. This might work if they are following the right behaviours and truly understand where they come from.

Unfortunately, all too often behaviours seen as successful are actually contrary to the behaviours the organisation believes it's trying to create throughout its culture. Having a set of values and behavioural statements only works when leaders consistently demonstrate them, not turn them on when under scrutiny.

But what if these behaviours are rewarded? Many businesses see the development of more 'damaging' behaviours – such as control, undermining expertise, acquiescing to the demands of a vocal bully – which all become the norm, due to the power base these behaviours create.

Every business at some point aims to create a set of behaviours which describe its values and use these behaviours as guidelines on 'how to behave'. I've been involved in many businesses where these behaviours are reviewed, measured and developed in the leadership population, with the intent of them becoming role models.

However, there's a clear sense of managed intervention here. It's based on the notion that if everyone falls into the framework, then 'good' behaviours and relationships will grow.

Why, then, is this rarely, if ever, the case?

Why do the managed change programmes which explain, instil and promote these behaviours, fail to get to the core of why people behave the way they do and continue to do so, despite frameworks to the contrary?

There must be something else going on which causes so many

people to fail to fully align with behavioural charters and feedback scores. It is surely linked to people's sense of authenticity.

If you're a leader of a business you own and have grown, you'll have a range of role models which may fall outside typical corporate structures. Or you may find you have no role models to follow and the idea of being a leader hasn't even entered your head.

Where does that leave you?

You'll most likely develop behaviours based on your memories of being managed in the past, or from information you've read or talked about.

Whilst these are useful sources of information, there's always a risk you'll create a way of operating not fully aligned with who you really are. When you add this to managing people, following someone else's model, it's likely to leave you vulnerable to inauthenticity, without knowing it.

Leaders and followers associate authenticity with sincerity, honesty, and integrity. It's the real thing: the attribute which uniquely defines great managers.

But while the expression of a genuine self is necessary for great leadership, the concept of authenticity is often misunderstood, not least by leaders themselves. They often assume authenticity is an innate quality, that a person is either genuine or not.

Some experts say authenticity is largely defined by what other people see in you. In their view, you can to a great extent, control it.

Becoming an authentic leader is a two-part challenge. You consistently have to match your words and deeds, otherwise followers will never accept you as authentic (or trustworthy).

To encourage people to follow you, you also have to get them to relate to you. To these experts this means presenting different faces to different audiences, a requirement which is hard to square with authenticity. Authenticity is not the product of manipulation, as this sounds. Instead it should accurately reflect aspects of the leader's inner self, so it can't be an act.

For this model to work, authentic leaders would need to know which personality traits they should reveal to whom and when. Highly attuned to their environments, authentic leaders rely on a combination of intuition and past experiences to understand the expectations and concerns of the people they seek to influence.

HOW DO WE KNOW WHO WE ARE?

To discover more about our authenticity, we typically look to understand more about ourselves.

To do this, we often turn to external measures and assessments, provided through psychometric tests. The most popular, such as Myers-Briggs Type Indicator [9](MBTI), Insights Discovery Personal Profile[10], DISC Personality Test[11] and Occupational

Personality Questionnaire[12] (OPQ) are used extensively in many areas of leadership and management development.

I've seen them used well as a tool to increase insight and self-awareness. Typically, they are based on theories of adult development which measure a degree of innate 'wiring' which makes us the way we are, plus a degree of learnt or developed behaviours from all stages and parts of our lives. In other words the nature and nurture mix.

Taking MBTI, as an example. The theory is, there are a number of traits which are present in us from birth (childhood), which are defined and paired as:

- Introversion/Extroversion
- Sensing/Intuition
- Feeling/Thinking
- Judging/Perceiving

Most development approaches suggest using an assessment tool to identify how your 'wired' preferences combine, to define your innate or natural core, which in that respect might be construed as a measure of your authentic self.

Certainly, our understanding of these traits or preferences are those which come most easily to us and are those that give us 'energy' provides great clues to what is authentic to us. But knowing your preferred or innate type is not enough.

In Myers and Briggs' model of development, they describe how, through adult phases of development, you should aim to develop behaviours more aligned to traits which don't naturally fall within your innate 'wiring'. To them, this gives you a wider repertoire of behaviours and helps you connect more effectively with others who have different type preferences.

The purpose of this is to open up more behaviours, which enables you to relate more easily to people with different traits to yourself. Being able to step outside your innate preferences and reach across to others through amending your behaviours is an essential way of building relationships.

There is an issue with this broadening of behaviours, as it can lead to individuals adopting behaviours they come to believe are naturally theirs, but which inherently take them away from being their authentic best.

When people see their behaviours working well in the world around them, there's a tendency to keep using them and believing they are the right way to operate. Typically, these behaviours will also be reinforced by those around us, who may naturally have those behaviours, as they will recognise them as similar to themselves and feel at ease.

Unfortunately, this is unlikely to be sustainable.

Either the individual will be 'found out' as others will realise the behaviours displayed are not authentic or natural, bringing us back to the trust factor. Also, the individual will find they run out of energy as it takes greater effort to operate with less natural behaviours.

In the worst case, the individual will be found out when they come across something which creates a stressed state. At this time, you can be sure they'll revert back to their natural preferences and leave some of those around them wondering what has changed and why.

For example, I had a client who was always describing himself as wrung out and exhausted after days filled with meetings and presentations. He came across as very outgoing, gregarious, and extroverted.

You would have been convinced he had scored highly on the extroversion scale in the MBTI. Amazingly, he scored the complete opposite – he displayed a high scoring introversion preference. When we dug a bit deeper into his profile and how he was finding his energy levels, it became clear he had learned early on in his business career that being introverted would potentially hold him back from being successful. So, he did just what Myers and Briggs recommended, developed some of the behaviours from the other traits which were not naturally his. He had developed very well-honed skills and behaviours in extroversion.

Of course, in doing so, he repeatedly operated outside his natural state. He took on the characteristics and behaviours of someone who was comfortable and at ease with continually expressing their thoughts and feelings in the moment. Over time, this left him exhausted and with a sense that he was fighting against the tide. I could feel the amount of effort he was putting in daily, just to sustain his portrayal as an extroverted person.

That's not to say those behaviours were wrong, but by continually operating outside his natural self, he was placing high demands on himself and moving further away from authenticity.

I'm not suggesting this client was trying to be inauthentic in doing this. He had taken on these characteristics so well that he himself would always describe himself as vocal, expressive and outgoing.

When we looked a bit deeper, however, he could only sustain these behaviours for a limited period of time before becoming tired. He described himself as always being on the edge of wanting to go away and be silent.

So many people who use assessments and models like MBTI get caught up in the label which becomes the defining feature of who they are. I've seen it used by some to excuse what they think they can't do and how they are different from everyone else.

For others, it's a huge relief being able to rationalise the collections of behaviours and no longer feel wrong or different from people around them. I remember being trained in MBTI and feeling a hit of excitement, that here at last was a way to help people get to the core of who they are and in doing so, move closer to that place.

However, the realisation I came to over time was very different. If it gave such insight and understanding and armed people with the tools they needed to develop broader behaviours and understand others, why then didn't it solve people's search for authenticity?

Another useful measurement tool, The Leadership Circle[12], aims to measure what they describe as inner and outer aspects of leadership.

The outer aspects are a selection of well-researched competencies (behaviours and skills) required for successful leadership, while the inner aspects relate to our assumptions, belief systems and behavioural habits which are created by our habitual thoughts.

Using their research, the creators of this instrument (Bob Anderson and his team), make an interesting link between the under or over-utilisation of certain competencies and the self-limiting beliefs held by the individual. Remember, the work by Kegan and Lahey (Immunity to Change) tried to do the same in relation to how assumptions get in the way of achieving goals.

In other words, whilst we all hold a broad range of skills and behaviours, how they are used in day-to-day life is determined by what we believe about ourselves and others' view of us.

For many, this creates a belief system based around the premise of 'How I have to be in the world', predicated on an unreal view of what we believe others think of us. This need for external validation leaves people in a place where their whole identity is tied up with how they believe they are perceived externally.

As you can imagine, from this place, it is more likely the behaviours an individual uses are based on fear, control or avoidance of external factors, rather than development of internally-driven fulfilment.

Many people remain at the adult development stage where this pattern creates the fear-based, avoidance behaviours you see. The Leadership Circle describes this as the 'reactive' phase. For many, being in this phase will show up as a cycle of reaction and action, which I believe all of us will recognise:

A problem or threat arises. This causes discomfort, which in turn makes you feel out of control and creates an inner conflict about what action should or shouldn't be taken. Remember, how this was described by Peters, as the work of the Chimp? At this point you are likely to react in order to attempt to get rid of the problem. The sense here is that if you can get rid of the problem, you will be free to get what you want.

Unfortunately, research indicates that this is never likely to be the case. Instead, a cycle of externally-driven 'issue-action-reaction' evolves, which becomes tiring and unfulfilling. These cycles form into common behavioural groups or patterns, called Reactive Leadership Styles.

In these reaction–action cycles, there are three groups of behaviours:

1. Controlling others
2. Behaviours which enable us to please or comply with others
3. Finally, behaviours aimed at protecting yourself

For me, this model helps explain some of the more extreme behaviours which have become more prevalent in the workplace over the last few years.

The need to be in control is a huge driver for many successful people in the workplace. This control extends outwards from themselves, to controlling everything around them. They have become so fearful of what might be 'found out' or in some way attacked, fearful of what will happen if any of the threads they hold so tightly slip or are taken way.

I once worked with a senior technology professional, who came into the organisation full of his past successes, which put people in a place of awe and admiration.

The stories created by this individual sounded so believable, it wasn't long before he gained further reinforcement by being given increased authority to make changes across his function. It was almost as if the spell of deceit had been cast over his peers and with it came the belief that anything he said was undeniably right.

What emerged as a result of this reinforcement was a prolonged period of destruction and denigration of all that existed before his arrival. He literally took apart everything which threatened or contradicted the way of leading he had come to believe was the only way.

He surrounded himself with 'trusted advisors' who created a further layer of control and external monitoring. They became the eyes and ears around his department and anyone found to be acting or talking against the new leader soon found themselves accused of misconduct through disciplinary process or dismissed.

As you can imagine, this created a culture of fear, resentment and stagnation. As a result, the organisation lost a large number of highly talented and forward-focused, transformational individuals. For the leader, this represented success, as a further removal of threat had been achieved, although in the long term, it proved detrimental to the organisation.

I found myself increasingly curious about how this person could yield so much power and why he found this mode of operating necessary.

Surely, creating an atmosphere of fear and acting as a bully cannot be the way this individual started life as a business leader?

From my work with adult development and leadership development models, it appeared this leader had, over the years, developed a range of behaviours in response to a high need for protection and security against feelings of vulnerability or insecurity.

If he had been assessed with the Leadership Circle tool, he would have scored highly in the 'controlling others' quadrant of the reactive leadership domain. Of course, what happens in these assessments is the individual cannot see how he is operating, whilst those around him who experience the effects of the behaviours will give feedback describing a very different experience. Often, an assessment like Leadership Circle is used to aid development by aiming to increase awareness in the individual about how he or she is experienced by those he or she works with.

However, this won't work when an individual's belief system generates further behaviours designed to eradicate anything seen as a threat to his or her knowledge, expertise and power.

This former colleague of mine created a belief that others in the workplace had to be managed and controlled. To him, they were the cause of the feelings of anxiety, fear and mistrust he experienced.

This leader came across as emotionally cold and lacking in empathy, when in fact he was likely to be living in his own reality saturated by other emotions (but kept well under wraps).

Set against Steven Peter's model of our brain structure and function – in particular, the Human brain and the Chimp brain – this type of destructive, over-controlling behaviour comes from the interplay between these two thinking parts of the brain.

The Human brain has a need to establish society and community. In each of us, it creates rules of behaviour, some of which are designed to manage the effects of the Chimp brain. It creates a sense of right or wrong based on the community's value judgements. The Human brain also strives to achieve happiness and success defined by the individual.

In this space, the Chimp becomes involved as part of the survival mechanism.

If a person has a need to 'succeed in business' the Chimp takes over this objective and seeks to protect the perceived status of the person. The Chimp does all it can to establish and protect its territory in the belief it must do this to ensure survival.

Unfortunately, the behaviours which emerge as a result of this primitive, instinctive mindset, actually lead to bullying and intimidation.

You can see how the inconsistent and irrational operations of the Chimp or emotional centre, seem entirely logical and correct when attached to a well-respected goal of success.

What you actually get is success at all costs, and the potential destruction of others who are perceived as a threat.

When you reflect on how much energy it must take someone to be in this state all day, every day, it's not surprising so many end up fuelled by adrenalin and exhausted by the relentless wariness required to deal with an attack.

In a way, according to Peter's model, people have lost the ability to manage the Chimp and it is running the show. What you see as the result is fear and insecurity becomes a self-fuelled cycle.

Going back to the Leadership Circle model, it is a useful tool to help people identify a picture of their behaviours patterns and what drives them.

What I appreciated when I used it, was the ability to see each person's true core values and the talents or gifts they already possess.

What you see is how the distorted pattern of the issue —action-reaction state cover these up and create the illusion of different values through different displayed behaviours.

For my bullying leader, whilst the gift couldn't be seen, as the more destructive outcomes had become so powerful, he is likely to have had an innate talent in creating clear plans and actions through others to successfully achieve outcomes. Unfortunately, this wasn't the 'gift' we experienced in the organisation.

WHAT'S IMPORTANT TO YOU?

When I ask clients to describe what's important to them, i.e. their values, it's easy to spot when something named as a value is in fact a set of behaviours. This often reinforces their existing thought patterns.

For example, I worked with a client and we used the Leadership Circle to assess the start point for our coaching. She scored highly in the area of complying. She tried to please everyone, sought consensus and tried hard to compromise her values in order to belong. The feedback she got from those around her was she was seen as a passive individual.

When we spoke more about what were some of her perceived drivers for these behaviours, she started by saying it was really important to her to 'get on with people'. She disliked conflict and felt it was always better to hear, understand and accommodate others' viewpoints, rather than impose her own.

When we looked deeper at the values she described, there was another power at play. It was clear she had a natural empathy, making her really tune in to people around her and understand their frailties and need for help.

However, over time, this innate gift was distorted as she used the complying behaviours more and more with people around her. In many important relationships, she clearly gained a great deal of reinforcement of how she was behaving. She regularly received praise and was seemingly able to head off very difficult situations, simply through her ability to find a solution which worked primarily for others.

Over time, this reinforcement made her believe this was the only way to succeed in life. On top of bringing reward, these behaviours had the added benefit of protecting her from fears and threats she saw in the negative behaviours of others.

This double reinforcement served to ingrain these pleasing, compromising and passive behaviours as her own and she adopted them as her core values.

What we unearthed alongside this thought was somewhat different. When we really looked at what was important to her, this client started to understand that when able to clear her head of old behaviours, her values were somewhat different.

She started to connect more readily with values around integrity, honesty and independence. She realised she could have all these values and still be gentle and compassionate, without the destruction of others and without harming relationships. The way she could embrace these values was more true to who she was than the value set she had developed in response to the perceived needs and wants of those around her.

As you can see unearthing values is no easy task. Even naming what's important to you, only takes you so far. What one person means when naming a value doesn't necessarily mean the same to another. Sometimes, changing the question around works to uncover a value. Ask yourself:

What's the one object; experience; or quality in life you couldn't do without? What are the qualities in the person you most admire in the world?

In trying to define values, what we aim to do is get closer to your authentic self. The part of you which comes from within, from your soul, rather than created by circumstances around you.

AN ALTERNATIVE APPROACH TO .... AUTHENTICITY

As mentioned earlier, I've seen many colleagues and clients who carry around layers of beliefs, assumptions and values adopted from others. Finding authenticity in yourself is a process of peeling away the layers of externally imposed views to discover your authentic self underneath. Using models, theories and frameworks or assessments can seem to help this process. They do reveal some level of detail which may lead to some moments of insight or clarity.

However, there's something missing in all these models.

When you look at measures and frameworks like the Leadership Circle you can see how they were created to deal with the effects of circumstances and events we have absorbed over the years and have allowed to shape us.

Let's take the complying and controlling behaviours we've

just looked at.

To me, these are behavioural habits or traits, which have developed in individuals through their experiences. It may be they were behaviours experienced as they were growing up or behaviours developed during their working life.

I'm sure you can remember starting your first job, how you consciously or sub-consciously watched your manager to see "how it was done around here". If your role model in these early, shaping years demonstrated a range of controlling-based management behaviours, it's more than likely you'll have developed some of these behaviours too. It's not to say you became controlling or complying. It's more likely it brought to the fore traits you already had and they became a little distorted as you emulated 'successful' behaviours.

For some, though, the opposite happens. It may be you consciously decided to develop opposite behaviours to ensure you're nothing like the role model you're with.

Either way, development of these behaviours, described as 'reactive', is based on our reactions to external experiences and events. These, in turn, create experiences (behaviours and feelings) which shape how we act.

Of course, our reactions to anything are defined by only one thing – the thoughts we create about an event.

If your personal thoughts tell you that being in control is good, safe and the best way to get things done, all your experiences are coloured by this. These thoughts become the dominant pattern or habitual setting from which you will create other thoughts and behaviours.

In the end, these thoughts form a sense of reality, where we see the world as if each thought were true. We, therefore, see the need to control or comply with people as an absolute state of reality to be achieved.

Set alongside this, in many of these leadership models, we're encouraged to move away from reactive behaviours to a more responsive framework.

Being responsive sets us up to stand back, take a broader view of any situation and decide on a course of action primarily designed to stop the 'issue-action-reaction' cycle.

However, one thing I know to be true is the development of responsive behaviours doesn't come through 'trying' to do or be something different. Instead, it comes through understanding we can access a higher level of awareness at any time, when we choose.

The move to, or the development of, more responsive behaviours signifies something quite different. It is the awareness that all experiences are the result of our own created thoughts. We generate a whole range of thoughts and we're able to choose which thoughts are most beneficial to focus on once we understand this is how the process works

Whilst we have focused on the behaviours which may or may not indicate someone's authenticity, there's more to being genuine, trustworthy and unique than just behaviours. Being authentic comes from our inner self, not the external manifestation so many models point to.

When you shed the experiences, memories and associated thoughts collected from the world around you, you realise your authenticity is already there waiting for you to re-discover it. There's nothing to be done, learned or developed.

I've already pointed you in the direction of our inner wisdom as the source of our innate being, the part of us which naturally balances and re-balances through all the circumstances and experiences of life.

To me, authenticity comes when we tap into that source of wisdom. It happens when we step away from the knowledge of what we think we need to have or be and from the endless searching for the 'right' way of doing or being.

We already know our core values, our core purpose and what gives us energy and what takes it away. All we have to do is stop being busy analysing and planning the corrective measures we think we need in order to be authentic. For many of us, though, we are stuck in a cycle of working hard to develop and grow. Of trying to eradicate 'bad behaviours' and find a new set of acceptable behaviours.

I know from my own personal experience:

1) This feels like hard work.

2) Whatever changes I manage to make often feel like they don't 'stick'.

What I've come to realise, and I hope you do too, is that it's not changing behaviours which makes change happen. It's changing our understanding of where thoughts are created and allowing ourselves the self-trust to know we can access our own innate wisdom at any time.

There are many examples around us where we have come to trust our understanding of a phenomenon and created new outcomes from this understanding. For example, gravity is a principle which has always existed and is always around us. Just because it wasn't understood, named or fully defined for hundreds of years, doesn't mean it wasn't there. It was, we just didn't understand it.

Once it was understood, we began to trust what it could do for us. Early attempts at flight in flimsy, small aircraft helped us understand the limits and mechanics of gravity. Today, we have huge, heavy aircraft flying long distances around the world because we understand gravity, its impact on objects. We have come to trust it to create an outcome we had once perceived to be impossible.

All we needed was to accept the understanding of the principle of gravity, understand the system it created and try new possibilities within that system.

Similarly, once we understand that we think, that we experience our thoughts and we are all part of a self-regulating system, which naturally return us to well-being and balance, we can trust the process of our life.

CHAPTER FIVE: DECISION-MAKING AND PROBLEM SOLVING

I've included decision-making in this book for one simple reason: there's a lot of discussion going on at the moment about what makes a great decision maker and how better decisions lead to greater success. This can only mean one thing: it's something researchers and developers are looking at to create a new model to aid the decision-making development of business leaders.

I've also included this for personal reasons. On projects I've worked on recently in larger organisations, I have been astounded by the evolution of decision-making into consensus-seeking. I have even trained people in one crucial part, of the decision–making process - the art of stakeholder engagement or management (depending on how gentle you want it to appear).

I have sat in many meetings, involving so many people from all over the world who all aim to participate in the decision-making process. As a result, there's few real decisions made, as appeasement and further analysis seem to be the preferred next steps.

Don't get me wrong, I'm all for discussion, sharing and engagement to ensure a good outcome. What I have struggled with is the endless waste of time and money taken by talking around issues and trying to seek solutions which meet everyone's needs. In terms of destroying businesses and creating meltdown, this one is right up there. For this and all the development time, energy and focus, I wanted to put this out there for scrutiny.

Developing problem solving skills is also a focus for many development programmes. Over the years, we have been provided with many creative thinking tools, designed to open up approaches to problem solving. The issue is, despite a world full of information and knowledge, there's more 'unknowns' than 'knowns'. Becoming an 'adaptive' leader, skilled at dealing with unknowns has been the focus of much leadership development over the last decade. Wherever there are development theories and methods, there's always the risk that instead of aiding business development, these methods will stifle and drown creativity in those seeking to develop it.

DECISION-MAKING

In researching the theories in this area, I recently read *Rework* by Jason Fried and David Heinemeier Hansson[13]. In the book, they offer a different approach to decision-making needed to build a business, based on their experiences of setting up their software company.

In one chapter, called *Decisions are Progress*, the authors suggest a great approach to decision-making: get on with it.

The problem they encountered was when decisions were delayed or ignored, they started to pile up. What they noticed was the tendency when faced with a pile of anything, is to reach a point where we act in a few narrow ways: deal with it too hastily, throw them out or continue to ignore the pile.

Their advice is to commit to making a decision and stop thinking about it. They argue that once you unlock this pattern, you get in the flow of decision-making, where each decision made is a foundation stone for progress.

Blockages and uncertainty arise when you put off making decisions in the hope a better solution will come tomorrow. Chances are, if you've no headspace for the decisions today, there won't be any more space tomorrow.

One great point the authors make was the need to manage the post-decision over-analysing. The reality is, even if you make a wrong decision in the moment, you don't have to live with the consequences forever, there'll be plenty more opportunities to make many more decisions. Even if a decision is wrong, it is still a step forward into action and creates a space for another decision right behind it!

Make sure you're not tied up by looking backwards critiquing and judging the decisions you've already made.

From the perspective of the authors, the power of success lies in creating progress, which feeds motivation and momentum.

These simple messages help us look in the right place to move ahead with decisions and making progress in business.

Others have decided to look at decision-making from a different place. For example, in studies by neuroscientists and summarised by David Rock in his book, *Your Brain at Work*[2] , there are clear physiological limitations at play in the brain which impact ability to make decisions. The mental processes used in decision-making take up considerable brain energy, which is a limited resource.

As all decision-making requires dealing with information, they recommend we stop trying to store information and create visuals and lists. This enables the brain to interact with information and reduces the energy consumed in the process. Making sure problem-solving tasks are attempted when the brain is fresh and fully stocked with energy, they say, will make the process much easier.

Steven Peters presents an interesting perspective on decision-making. In many circumstances, making a decision involves dealing with a lot of new and unknown factors.

For the Chimp part of the brain, this is likely to trigger the survival instinct as a response to a perceived threat to your safety. The Chimp aims to offer you three possible responses of fight, freeze or flight as a way out of the situation.

However, if none of these three actions are chosen, indecision creeps in and the Human part of your brain tries to delay the choice by looking for more facts or evidence. When this happens, an even stronger response kicks in. Your body will release adrenalin and the Chimp part of your brain will start to generate negative thoughts, creating a high degree of anxiety. Unfortunately, this fuels itself, as the Chimp brain counteracts the reassurance from the Human brain by generating even more catastrophic thoughts.

You'll recognise these:

"What if it all goes wrong?"

"You'll look a fool, a failure".

"What if you get found out you're not really the person everyone thought you were....?"

As a result, a series of brain-generated processes will lead to greater and greater of levels indecision. When your physiology is affected through chemicals such as adrenalin and cortisol, it becomes harder for your brain to sort and manage facts.

If, as Peters says, the Chimp brain is always in a state of constant vigilance, feeling under threat with every perceived danger, the emotional responses associated with fear and insecurity are the first to surface.

What's clear is they do little or nothing to help the situation. Not knowing the solution or the right decision will not be sorted out by an anxiety-led reaction. Rather the degree of fear it triggers only serves to increase the paralysis and indecision stresses many of us know.

What does good decision-making look like?

Many people cite the late Steven Jobs as the ultimate, innovative decision-maker. He is seen as someone who evaluated information quickly and often stepped over the edge, taking risks with such strong self-belief, he became someone leaders aspired to.

The truth, now heavily reviewed after his passing, seems rather different.

Joe Nocera of the New York Times said this of Jobs:

".....violated every rule of management. He was not a consensus-builder but a dictator who listened mainly to his own intuition. He was a maniacal micromanager. He had an astonishing aesthetic sense, which business people almost always lack. He could be absolutely brutal in meetings: I watched him eviscerate staff members for their "bozo ideas." . . . He never mellowed, never let up on Apple employees, and never stopped relying on his singular instincts in making decisions about how Apple products should look and how they should work."

It's interesting to note although Jobs' personal style was often harsh and certainly seemed to go against typical leadership traits of openness, listening and empathy, he overcame this by his singular and unrelenting focus on a few projects or products.

In listening to his intuition he allowed his own inner guide to unfold what the next steps should be. That's not to say he would shut out other possibilities. Apparently, he was always willing to change a course of action if challenged and if he felt the alternative offered a better way forward. It appears having a continual link to his core instincts gave him the foresight and courage to make bold steps and fast decisions.

In effect, he disengaged his Chimp and his Human brain – both of which required too much time and attention – and was prepared to move forward without the need for self-protection or a quantity of evidence. In a recent article in *Fortune*, Bill Clinton was asked what attributes are shared by great leaders. He, like Jobs, pointed to the need to be steadfast in pursuit of a goal, but being flexible in the approach to achieving it. Clinton highlighted the following attributes:

- Courage to make hard decisions and the confidence to stay with them
- The common sense to listen to others and involve them
- The strength to admit when you have made a mistake
- Being able to trust others and trust your instinct alongside your intellect
- Be able to compromise and know the lines you cannot cross

As you can see there's a picture building which shows how all the foundations of knowing yourself come together to support key leadership and business activities.

You can't have authenticity without trust. You can't make great decisions unless you have trust in yourself and others.

The models of success as a leader, point to types of behaviour and a degree of knowledge, but there are some which show something more instinctive is at play.

DEALING WITH THE UNKNOWN

Nowadays, we have access to vast amounts of information, all of which are designed to help evaluate next steps; appraise steps we have taken; inform decisions and solve problems.

Steven Peters is clear about how knowledge and facts are used by the Human brain and its processes. In managing the emotional, inconsistent and often chaotic Chimp brain, Peters explains the Human brain reverts to use of facts and evidence as the basis for making decisions and plans.

David Rock and neuroscientists who focus on leadership behaviours, have identified theories on how our brain operates to make decisions. From a neuroscience perspective, identifying problems is a lot easier than finding solutions.

Problems are events or circumstances we have seen before; it's how we know they are problems in the first instance. We can go to our memory and find mental maps similar to the problem, which help define what the problem is.

It gets trickier when we need to find a solution. From a brain perspective, solutions, by their nature, are likely to be events or activities we've never seen or experienced before. Trying to visualise something for which we don't have a mental map is difficult for the brain.

When you apply this to decision-making or even achieving goals, you can see why this is so tricky.

Goal setting requires you to visualise a situation you may never have seen or experienced before. Even if we have previously experienced our desired situation, the fact is, humans are bad at forecasting how we *will* feel, and we end up defining the future based on how we feel today. Humans find it difficult to create a future emotional or mental state.

By becoming more aware of our physiological limitations and understanding why we find certain types of brain processes difficult, Rock suggests we can start to modify our behaviours. In doing so, he suggests, we'll be able to modify our brain's ability to process information and improve our ability to deal with many more required solutions.

Decision-making is similar. With access to so much information, it's commonplace for people to base decisions only on known facts. However, despite access to a wealth of knowledge, the pace of change and increasing complexity in the world means there is more we *don't* know than we *do* know.

It has become difficult for many leaders to admit they don't know which solution to follow or even, sometimes, which problem to solve. Given the human brain's desire to work on what is known against what is unknown it's understandable it feels tough.

CREATING AGREEMENT NOT CONTROL

For a business or team leader, it often falls to them to create the direction or vision to enable everyone to focus in the same place and use their energies to the right purpose.

However, as touched on already, I hear from business leaders how hard it is to create a vision for the future when the pace of change is so fast and there is so much uncertainty:

- How do you set a course for the future when so much is unknown in the present?
- How can anyone predict where they or the business will be in five years?

After all today, there are so many businesses which don't even exist (when five years ago their long-term strategy wasn't exactly to be out of business!).

I've seen business leaders and their employees so weighed down by the task of creating a robust strategy, the process of creating it brings out more conflict and misunderstanding than any lack of vision could ever cause.

If you remember, from earlier in this section, the physiology of the brain makes it essential for a vision or direction to be simple, clear and concise. Having to process detailed descriptions of a vision not only burdens the brain with unbalanced, energy-taking processing, but adds to the risk of misinterpretation and misaligned thinking. Our brains find it difficult to predict unknown states and how we might feel, so we rely on current or known experiences to create an impression of what the future might be like.

I'm not saying a simple vision automatically drives all of us to think and act in the same way. For this to be the case, we'd work on the premise all of us think and act in the same way in response to the same external event or information.

For every one of us in business, this is simply not the case. You cannot coerce or force people into thinking a certain way.

However, I do believe to create alignment behind a goal or vision is a lot simpler than many business consultants might have you believe, if you approach it from the right place.

Let's take an example.

All employees of Nordstrom follow the Nordstrom vision: Nordstrom is all about exceptional customer service. It's a really clear statement. But it still allows each employee to add their own interpretation to how this plays out on a day-to-day basis.

Each function, team and customer assistant in the store, moment-by-moment creates thoughts on what exceptional customer service means to them.

Some thoughts may generate a sense of something less than exceptional, such as:

"I'm tired today..."

"I wish all these customers would go away..."

"Why do they have to be so demanding?"

However, the clear intent of the vision creates a shared check and balance, so it's more likely employees choose to follow more positive, aligned thoughts such as:

"As long as this customer leaves happy, I've done a good job."

"I'll help this customer find the right dress to ensure she leaves satisfied."

Having employees putting their energy, experience and behaviours behind the more positive, aligned thoughts, creates the kind of outcomes any business needs.

No matter what it might feel like, no business wants its people to feel unclear, stressed, overwhelmed or directionless. There are so many studies showing how detrimental these emotional states are to productivity.

However, what isn't needed is control.

Having alignment or agreement is not about controlling the thoughts of people in the business.

Unfortunately, many businesses set up employee development and performance programmes with the view they can do just that. These programmes rely on the belief that by creating clear reward or punishment consequences for actions or behaviours, employees come to understand how they need to act to be successful.

In reality, these are simply externally-driven processes, which never in their own right change the way an individual employee thinks, feels or behaves.

Where you see such processes work it is really only by default, when the individual's own thoughts happen to align with the outcomes the programmes are trying to achieve.

In other words, if an employee allows the creation of positive thoughts about the targets he or she has been set, or the role to be performed, this translates into positive behaviours, which are rewarded through a performance management process. It isn't the process itself creating the outcome.

These processes work on the misunderstanding that by changing or controlling our responses to events, circumstances or information, all employees become more positive in how they work and more productive in what they deliver.

What's interesting is that changing situations or circumstances does not create change in people. Neither does attempting to instil a more positive way of operating – this is an 'outside in' approach to building alignment and productivity.

By actively setting out to make people feel more positive and productive, you are in effect creating more distractions for them to focus their thoughts on, rather than simply setting out a clear road ahead.

Only real change, despite reward and punishment consequences, comes when each individual realises they create their thoughts and therefore their own experience. They can then choose which thoughts are valid, which are worth following and which are emotional reactions; more likely to cause a destructive set of behaviours.

What does this mean?

As we know from the work of neuroscientists, when we accumulate experiences, they are stored as memories or reference maps. We use these maps to help us understand the world around us. By developing these experiences from a different source, you can see how the knock-on effect shifts how we reference or map events around us.

Simply knowing how we individually create our thoughts, which lead to behaviours and feelings, puts us firmly in the driving seat. By relaxing, accessing a sense of calm and letting go of the need to 'try' to change, we'll find ourselves in a new place over time but without so much effort, stress and anxiety.

Calm is just one thought away from chaos.

Calmness is a natural outcome from encouraging your true self.

A calm state of mind comes from within.

Just as you can create thoughts of turbulence and overwhelm, you can create calm and head space. No amount of control, management or rewards from outside yourself will make this happen. It comes from within you.

THE VALUE OF INSIGHT

Both Clinton's view of leadership attributes and Jobs' reported use of insight make it worth a closer look. Insight is something we all experience and know the value of. We may call it instinct, intuition or 'gut feel', but whatever the name, it's a real experience, even if we don't always realise at the time.

In physiological terms, it's been discovered that at the moment of insight, a burst of fast brain waves, all firing together, occurs. This creates an energy surge, magnified by a rush of adrenaline and dopamine and, as a result, we feel great and our attention stays focused on this new piece of information.

While this moment has a short physiological footprint with the neurochemical cocktail wearing off fast, it's important to quieten the mind to allow more of these moments of insight to be noticed.

Insight is always available but not always realised. By quietening the mind, I don't mean taking overt, action steps to go about trying to reduce thoughts. This in itself, becomes a distraction, removes focus and involves 'doing'. You end up looking externally for ways to access insight, which may or may not work, but it is looking at the wrong process. It's like thinking umbrellas cause rain, simply because every time it rains there are umbrellas around.

Insight is the moment when, what you already know from your own innate wisdom, pops to the surface through your conscious mind.

It's exactly the opposite of knowing or doing more. For insight to be heard, you've got to be doing and knowing less, to create the space for insight to emerge.

I'm sure you've experienced the moment when a solution to a problem suddenly pops into your head. It's usually when you're relaxed, focused on something else and in a 'dreaming' state. You may recognise this from being on holiday, when you're out for a long relaxing walk, or even just lying in the bath.

I can hear you saying it's not possible to be in this state every day with your time already filled with so much to do or think about. I totally recognise this but I believe once you understand where thought is coming from, you'll experience the shift to enable you to create the internal environment which connects you to insight more frequently. Remember my example about the principle of gravity. Once we came to understand the principle and how the systems around it worked, we have created outcomes, previously believed to be impossible.

When you truly understand that thoughts move 'through you' and don't happen 'to you', it's easier to understand that thoughts do not need to be controlled or managed. Letting go of this need frees up space and focus, creating the space you need to access your innate wisdom and notice these insights.

I believe insight is the direct result of being connected to your spiritual core. Even if moments of insight are only fleeting and are quickly submerged by personal thoughts and experiences, it's still always there in the background. We must always be connected... how could we not be? The moment of insight should be noticed and treasured and provide the realisation there's always more available when needed.

THE OVERWHELM OF PROBLEM-SOLVING STRATEGIES

For businesses today, there is a clear need for good decision-making and creative problem-solving. What happens in response, is the development of a raft of strategies and interventions, designed to eradicate unknowns and fill the space with knowledge and tactics.

Take for example, stakeholder management. Its use has increased across business as an effective strategy for predicting and managing the relationships and reactions of those around you. The idea is that if you can manage stakeholders, you gain some control over how they respond to issues, changes or problems you're involved with.

I've been in organisations which use complex analysis and mapping processes designed to provide detailed insight into what 'might' happen and what is an 'influencer' on each stakeholder.

The use of these strategies and techniques will only take you so far and yet, in business, they are seen as the way to develop capability, change behaviours and master the art of decision-making. Even the greater understanding of brain physiology, has created a raft of new steps to take, new ways to structure time and new ways to think. By following all these, where will you be?

Faster, focused and a better problem-solver or overwhelmed by the need to follow the correct process to 'get it right'?

AN ALTERNATIVE APPROACH TO....DECISION-MAKING

As you might anticipate, creating systems for management and control don't sit well with me as an effective approach to better decision-making or problem-solving. Equally, creating mechanisms for knowing more and trying to foresee problems before they arise through predictive thinking, does not lead to the results you desire.

Holding knowledge signifies a risk of cluttering your thinking which does not help when making decisions. Put a few people in the room who have all the knowledge they think they need, and all the thoughts they've created and you'll get a lot of 'noise'.

No wonder meetings can be fraught with endless discussion and consensus but very little progress. After all, in this context, who has the headspace to truly hear and understand everything being said?

With these approaches you end up with an increase in personal thoughts, which ultimately constrains decision-making, due to the over-processing and emotional responses triggered when the emotional centres of the brain take hold.

Equally, no matter how much we think we can anticipate how others will react to a situation, the reality is, we have no idea what they are thinking. We are only likely to see or be at the receiving end of, their experience of their thoughts. And guess what? We will only be able to base our experience of this on the thoughts we then create in response.

For me, it's a cycle which doesn't serve to move anyone through a better decision-making process.

I'd suggest time and energy would be better spent following the lead laid out by Jobs. By accessing his intuition and tuning into his 'singular instincts', he demonstrated something valuable. He didn't need to know more, he didn't aim to predict, he was able to trust his ability to access his own inner wisdom.

He also did something that many of us are told and few of us do – be prepared to really listen to others and be prepared to hear what they propose.

We listen with a view to persuading, proving wrong or in some way judging. Jobs showed the value of listening to hear the wisdom of others. When he demonstrated the value of this collective innate ability to solve problems, he showed no-one needs to know all the answers.

There's enough inner wisdom to go round.

CHAPTER SIX:
DEALING WITH MOODS AND MINDSET

One thing we all experience is the shifting of our emotions and moods. We can start a day feeling fantastic then suddenly it seems a cloud has descended and things start to look less positive, for no apparent reason.

Having low moods are a fact of life in all of us as humans. We can't expect to be 'happy' or eternally upbeat all day, every day.

As we've seen, in work such as Peters', dealing with emotions is an important part of success in life.

Later, I'll take a broader look at emotional intelligence, but for now, it seems worth looking at the impact of emotions on how we think and perform in life.

When our emotional centre becomes dominant, it feels hard – if not impossible – to move to a more measured, constant state. The spiral of thinking, which takes hold when we are in a low mood takes us down to feelings of hopelessness, loss, lack of self-esteem and feelings of being the victim to the circumstances around us.

It's easy to believe the world has been cruel and poor luck or judgement is to blame. In response, people aim to go deeper and fix all the 'problems' they see, believing when they do, everything will be better.

Others become caught up in the need to fix their external environment and become aggressive or bullying in their desire to change what they believe is happening to them because of it.

At times like this, events and circumstances can take us down to a lower state of being. The death of a loved one or the loss of a job, will naturally leave us feeling sad, grieving for what has been lost and longing for the return of what we had before.

What happens in this state requires a bit more understanding.

In the traditional theories, low moods, anxiety or even depression are seen as states to be corrected through active intervention. Such intervention might involve drugs to re-balance the brain chemistry, Cognitive Behavioural Therapy (CBT or Talking Therapy) or psychiatric analysis and treatment. Often the focus of the therapies is to look back at the events seen as the root cause of the issues presenting repeatedly.

For example, there was a recent study which found people who had been bullied as children were much more likely to have mental illness, such as depression well into adulthood, even up to 40 years later. (BBC, April 14, 2014).

Whilst I'm not going to review the world of mental illness, it's an important area to be touched upon, as so many businesses lose many hours of employee time through time off due to depression, stress or anxiety disorders.

It's an area many HR departments tackle through work-based programmes. These range from the provision of stress management programmes, to adding mental health services to employee benefits programmes. It is certainly seen as something to be 'fixed' to aid business performance and ensure employee well-being.

While it's clear low moods affect many of us at some point, what's not clear is how some people respond to life events by moving into a low or depressed place, while others move through these events with a more positive outlook.

If an individual event leads to the creation of thoughts and the experience of these through feelings, there must be a point at which we will either choose to continue allowing our prevalent mood to remain low, or allow our thinking to shift and create a different mood state.

There are some people who, when faced with a major event, such as loss of a job or decline of a business will find themselves in a perpetual state of feeling low about it. They start every day with the black hand of depression or anger hanging over them. They come to believe it is natural to feel that way, day-in day-out.

After all, how could they feel happy or content in the face of something so devastating?

When someone remains in this state, I believe they move from a short term reaction, to an event created by their thought, to a long term response. They believe they experience a low mood because of what that has happened to them.

Conversely, there are those who experience the same catastrophic event, feel a short-term dip in their mood, but move on more readily with a positive mindset.

So, what's the difference?

How can two people have such different outcomes?

To explain the difference, traditional therapies and even change management models, would have us look at the individual's 'wiring' – what they've experienced in the past and their capacity to respond rather than react to an event. This only takes our understanding so far.

Traditional approaches are still pointing to an event as the on-going cause of how an individual feels. Typically, we work to unravel and analyse our reactions, then create a strategy to shift to a more positive mood or mindset.

Therapeutically, this may look like anti-depression drugs or psychiatric support. In the work environment it may take the form of training or coaching an individual, to shift awareness and move to a different pattern of action.

As I've said before, this is likely to lead to a temporary fix. By attempting to either change circumstances or our reaction to the circumstances, we're not looking in the right place for a solution to low moods.

What really makes the difference in how someone reacts to an event is their thinking.

If a person sees themselves as generating thought, as therefore being able to move through thoughts without intervention, this gives them more scope to handle difficult situations. It becomes clear that only their thoughts can create a low mood and unpleasant experience.

It's not to say if you know you are creating thoughts, you'll never experience low moods or a less positive mindset. If this were the case, we could no longer call ourselves human.

Experiencing emotions arising from our thoughts is what makes us the feeling beings we are.

When we shift our paradigm, it's possible to understand having a low mood is not a perpetual state. We have the capacity to experience low moods and understand the natural re-balancing of our state allows us to move through these. We just need to allow the balancing system to work, rather than trying to intervene.

Once we trust the natural ebb and flow of life, we know every low mood-generating thought is eventually replaced by a series of higher mood-generating thoughts. It's only when we feel we must intervene, fix or manage thoughts, we end up disturbing our natural self-correcting process.

It's not to say if you lose your job, your feelings of helplessness or despair arising from thoughts focused on loss or the future aren't valid or feel real. Of course they are.

The fork in the road becomes clear when the thoughts continue and deepen, taking the form of:

"It's not fair."

"Why have I been singled out?"

"I'm always subject to bad luck..."

"I'll never get another job..."

An individual may get stuck in an exhausting spiral of low mood thinking. Or an individual can start to shift their thinking to:

"This may provide an unexpected opportunity."

"I might be able to create something new and better."

"I wasn't fulfilled in that role and I can now be free to find something else."

The understanding you can access natural re-balancing, whilst not providing an immediate solution, will take you to more creative positive outcomes. When not consumed by a spiral of personal thoughts and experiences, you are more likely to be able to find (hear) the wisdom coming from within, which shows you the way forward.

An individual stuck in a mindset of helplessness in the face of external events, who creates a powerful downward cycle, will find it much harder if not impossible, to create enough space to find the way forward. They will be more caught up in the story they believe is reality rather than creating a new, more positive reality through allowing insightful thinking. How many times have you thought that a certain situation was the most devastating thing to ever happen to you, only later to realise this was a perfect course of events and the lesson you needed right then?

IMPACT OF EMOTION ON BUSINESS

Given everyone is a feeling human being, you can assume emotions have a significant impact on business.

If it wasn't something considered to be "getting in the way of success" there wouldn't have been so much time and effort devoted to understanding and managing it. The need to manage people and change, has led to the development of processes, systems and theories – all with the aim of supporting and controlling people as they experience emotional reactions.

In business change management approaches, dealing with people and change is seen as the most difficult challenge. There's an avoidance of dealing with the 'people' side of change, due to fear of dealing with the emotions arising from it.

It is often said, it's not change itself that's difficult; it's the fear and anxiety caused by change which creates the challenge.

I've worked on numerous large scale programmes, all of which involved some degree of change for employees in the business. I've worked with management and leadership teams, all fearful of the challenge of changing people, whether it is to positively embrace a new system, a new structure or new way of working.

Alongside the broader change management models, such as Kotter's 8-step programme or Lewin's change model, I've already mentioned, there are many models used to explain how people respond to change. I've used the DERAC model associated with grief to describe the process an individual goes through in dealing with change.

DERAC describes each stage in the process as follows:

D = denial

"It's not happening to me". Avoidance or distraction in the hope it goes away.

E= emotion

Here's where anger, fear, despair or sadness come to the surface. How people react and display these emotions may vary day-to-day, even hour-by-hour.

R = response (react)

This is when the individual decides to take action to deal with the change. This may be more avoidance, aiming to increase their understanding or removing themselves from the situation as far as possible.

A = acceptance

Here the person gradually comes to terms with the change. They realise no matter what, the change and effects of change are inevitable. They stop fighting and creating obstacles and start to soften a little in their approach.

C = change

Here is where the individual starts to behave differently and embodies the change.

A descriptive process like DERAC has helped many understand their own emotional reactions to change and those in others. It is described as a non-linear process, where you can move between stages in a variable pattern. Knowing where you are in a process, fulfils a need of applying logic and structure to the chaotic and inconsistent world of emotion. In Peters' model, it's something the Human brain might use to manage the activities of the Chimp.

AN ALTERNATIVE APPROACH TO .... MOODS AND MINDSET

Obviously, a process such as DERAC does not exist unless it is founded in thought.

A person will only be said to be at the Denial stage when they are creating thoughts focused on denying the change is real.

Interestingly, in business change management, the process is often used as the foundation of managing people through change, as if the process itself could govern the experience.

You can see Denial will be deepened and may last longer if an individual's thoughts are focused on the event being 'done to them'. They may use past habits of behaviour, which may have proved successful before, to create a perceived sense of safety and make them believe no change is happening. The person is using their thoughts to create their own reality, their own version of the situation. Of course, we do this all the time, but in this case, the version of reality is hooked into past experiences – thoughts, emotions and behaviours.

You can see how the Emotion stage becomes the response to these thoughts and this version of perceived reality. Whether the emotion is a short term experience or a long term mindset, again, depends on understanding where thoughts and reactions are created. Thoughts are not created by the event or the change, they can only be created by the individual. I would normally add to this 'in response to the event they are experiencing' but this is also not true. Thoughts can be created or not created and have nothing to do with the event. For instance, I can believe my partner is having an affair when it's not happening.

Do you see the difference?

When moving to Reactions, how a person behaves is linked to their understanding of the process of thoughts. If the thoughts created are negative, it's more likely a pattern of more damaging reactions will arise. A person may move to primitive reactions of fight, flight or freeze at the simplest level.

If this happens a person can become trapped in a fear-based pattern of thought, and deeper feelings-based actions arise in an attempt to fight back against what's happening.

Of course, if the thinking is negative, there is greater potential for the reactions to be more negative.

Understanding we each create our own version of reality, gives us more scope to let go of more negative or destructive thoughts and reactions. It allows us to let these flow through us, allowing more space and focus on re-balancing thoughts and positive outcomes.

In this way, Acceptance is reached a lot sooner by someone open to the natural flow and re-balancing of the system, which brings the experience to a self- regulated state. In this way, acceptance cannot be achieved through external intervention or coercion.

The final stage, Change, can only be fulfilled when one thing happens – the individual allows their thoughts to change. This doesn't happen through effort but through hooking into the awareness and insight available to them at all times through the intelligence of the system.

When an individual realises they and they alone have the power/ capacity to allow their thoughts to change, letting go of personal, habitual thoughts and embracing thought drawn from the endless source of inner wisdom, they then step into a new way of being. Having an uncluttered mind is an important role in enabling this to happen.

Having knowledge about these stages of change does nothing but add further thought to a person's mind and keep them further away from a clear, re-balanced state, where they can access all the understanding they need to deal with change around them.

In effect, what mapped out change processes like DERAC or Kotter's 8-step change management approach do is take your focus away from the way ahead.

One way to see this is in an example written by the spiritual teacher, Mooji[14]. He describes how, when learning to drive, a new driver is out in rain for the first time. The instructor tells him to put on the windscreen wipers to clear away the raindrops on the screen.

In response, the new driver starts to panic, saying that he can't possibly drive with the wipers on as all he can do is follow the wipers with his eyes, instead of being able to focus on the road ahead. The instructor calmly tells him to look through the action of the wiper blades and remain focused on the road.

The new driver continues to panic, with the car veering all over the road as his focus follows the movement of the blades. Only when he is able to ignore the action of the blades and shift his focus back to the road ahead, will he drive a straighter, safer path.

This is a great metaphor for what happens when people focused on the framework or model and the thoughts arising from these. These thoughts are distractions, as were the wiper blades, causing the person to lose focus on the way ahead and instead struggle to remain on the safest path ahead.

If we follow all the thoughts entering our head, from whatever external source, we find it hard to see the way ahead and become disorientated, panicked and confused, struggling to regain a steady state.

Adding more sources of information, development and learning programmes into any business, creates this effect. You and your people will be distracted by external frameworks, the thoughts these create and the feelings which develop as a result.

As we know from brain physiology, we don't need to fill our minds with any more information. The only information anyone needs is to understand where thoughts are created and the power of letting thoughts come and go, to clear space for true understanding to be heard.

CHAPTER SEVEN:
EMOTIONAL INTELLIGENCE

I heard the expression the other day about "walking in someone else's shoes". It struck me how much we aspire to do this, yet what an impossibility it is.

To understand this let's start by looking at one of the best-known ways to understand your own emotional awareness and ability to understand other's worlds: emotional intelligence.

This summary is simply an overview, not a complete guide. I'm using it to provide a method of understanding about how useful these models are in shaping our thinking and behaviours.

When the concept of emotional intelligence was first developed in the 1990s, it felt like a massive step forward. It described a unique kind of intelligence, different from the usual measure of cognitive intelligence or IQ. Here, at last, was a framework for people to increase their awareness of themselves and each other.

Daniel Goleman, one of the foremost drivers of this theoretical framework, who in 1998 described emotional intelligence as:

"The capacity for recognising our own feelings and those of

others, for motivating ourselves and for managing emotions well in ourselves and in our relationships"

Taking this a little further, Reuven Bar-On who created his model of Social and Emotional Intelligence, describes emotional intelligence as:

"..emotional-social intelligence as a cross section of interrelated emotional and social competencies, skills and facilitators that determine how effectively we understand and express ourselves, understand others and relate with them and cope with daily demands"

There are some commonly agreed facts about emotional intelligence (EQ).

The behaviours and components which make up EQ can change over time (similar to the theory underpinning Myers-Briggs' 16 preferences). It is not a measure of personality, although it does build personality traits. It does not describe aptitude, predict academic performance or point to any particular vocational interest.

The model of emotional intelligence is described by four quadrants, each of which contains a number of measured dimensions and so can be used in assessment as well as development.

These quadrants are:

	SELF	OTHERS
AWARE	Emotional awareness	Empathy
MANAGE	Stress management (self-regulation)	Adaptability (Relationship management)

EMOTIONAL AWARENESS

Looking at this quadrant, you can see how much emphasis is placed on knowing more about yourself through understanding your feelings and the causes of them. This stance reflects the widely-held view that the more insight and analysis you can perform in getting beneath the surface of feelings, to find root causes and triggers, the better able you are in managing those feelings.

Personally, I've spent years working through all the events, experiences and memories from childhood to now. Identifying all the feelings associated with those events, in an attempt to understand what drives my behaviours.

It's a really interesting exercise and certainly could take up a lifetime of analysis. So, what about when you 'know' what event might have formed a memory, which may then be retrieved as a thought and which might explain a series of feelings and behaviours you experience now? What do you do, then?

Typically, this where therapy comes in. You and your therapist may work through a range of tools and techniques deigned to shift, change or eradicate a particular thought-behaviour pattern.

Unfortunately, that's where the cycle of analysis, judgement and self-improvement becomes all-consuming and takes up vital 'headspace'. In doing so, it blocks you from tuning in to what's really driving the process you're caught up in.

What is really powerful about this quadrant is the way it points to your sense of purpose. I'm not sure tying the concept to self-improvement and roadmaps, quite allows for the natural realisation of your purpose. But acknowledging the power of the purpose in your emotional well-being is a great place to start.

EMPATHY

In this quadrant, the emphasis is on how well an individual uses their own emotional awareness to create good relationships with others. These are detailed in the following dimensions:

Empathy – the ability to read the emotions of others and show care and concern for them.

Social Responsibility – which centres on being a constructive, contributing member of a social group and being able to do things with and for others (in other words, not selfish).

Interpersonal Relationship – which focuses on feeling at ease in social situations and being able to establish and maintain positive relationships.

This quadrant starts to move us towards an understanding of ourselves in relationship with others. Later, I will touch on the need for positivity and productivity as the basis for great teams and successful relationships. For me, the empathy quadrant starts to describe some of these factors.

It's here the ability to "stand in another's shoes" really comes home. We are encouraged to develop empathy and patterns of behaviour to support relationships with others; I have no argument with that.

What bothers me is the belief that somehow I'm able to really understand the reality created by another person.

As each person creates their own thoughts, which in turn creates their own view of reality, how can anyone else aim to truly understand what their reality looks like? For me, it is only *they* who can see and, to a limited extent, understand that reality.

I cannot see it *with* them, as I would be viewing their world through my eyes and perceptions. Typically, empathy at this level requires us to interpret someone else's expressed feelings or behaviours. The only way we can do this is through our own understanding of the framework of thoughts, memories and experiences. Therefore, the interpretation automatically becomes tainted by our own frame of reference.

How can we stand in their shoes without stepping on their toes?

There is much value in connecting with people without trying to interpret or predict their thoughts. To do this you need to listen deeply, to take you beyond hearing the story, the words and the logic they use, as these draw you into their 'outside in' way of thinking.

Instead, by suspending your own need to 'fix, heal or find a solution' and just listening to what the other person says, you will create a compassionate space where they can show you who they are and all that they know, from the 'inside out'.

By all means, stand alongside them to notice and hear where they are, but do so in a bigger pair of shoes. No toe squashing required.

STRESS MANAGEMENT (SELF-REGULATION)

Two dimensions in this quadrant look at how you manage stress when it's from two sources:

Stress tolerance – which focuses on how you cope with stress created by external events. Also, how well you hold the belief you can control and influence the problem and outcome, while maintaining a positive attitude.

Impulse control – which is linked to the concepts of self-discipline and self-awareness. In this dimension, the focus is on the ability to control emotions, resist impulses and maintain self-control.

I'm very aware many leaders today believe they have the tools to master stress management. We're bombarded by ways to manage the impact of external events on our emotional well-being. You only need to look at the rise of mindfulness and meditation in mainstream Western society, to see the extent of the need.

Finding a way to tolerate stress may even be a reason why you're reading this book, as we look in many places for the answer. When I created the Headspace Company to help tackle stress, I knew so many business leaders were working very hard to understand the causes of stress and find some magical way of controlling it.

The fact is, managing stress through a range of techniques generally seems to give only temporary relief. A few people find peace or calm for a few minutes a day through meditation, deep breathing, or other mindfulness techniques.

What such techniques can do, though, is create more thoughts than you're trying to eradicate. Simply by thinking you 'need' to meditate has you worrying about finding the time, the best place to it, the best way to do it, etc. It's hardly head-emptying stuff.

If you're like me, even when you try to meditate, your mind is so hooked on 'being useful', it fails to join the 'mindfulness party' and carries on processing, finding solutions to possible future events and keeping you switched on for any eventuality.

Adding a new technique does not actually change the fundamental principle that stress, anxiety and overwhelm come from the thinking your personal, ego-based mind generates. In fact, overwhelm often comes from the sheer amount of thought generated at any one time.

These end up blocking the natural healing and re-balancing

processes which see you through difficult spells. If your head is so full of thinking based on past events, future fears and possibility, the real source of wisdom has no space to be seen or heard.

In his book *Do Nothing!*, Damian Mark Smyth[15] sheds an entirely new light on the search for the best stress management method. As the title suggests, he advocates a different approach to overwhelm: do nothing.

This doesn't mean sit or wallow in your negative thoughts, as this only creates more. He suggests doing nothing based on 'letting go'. This means you stop trying to find the answer to your current state by working hard to change the events or people around you.

If you take time out from the relentless push to 'find the right way' and relax, slow down and notice what's already there, you'll find your internal system automatically finds a way to re-balance to its natural state. It's from this state your authenticity and your true self is able to lead the way, rather than the habitual thinking patterns generated by your mind.

ADAPTABILITY

This quadrant of emotional intelligence looks at adaptability and your ability to change in response to people and circumstances around you. It also includes problem solving, your ability to identify problems and generate solutions

This obviously encompasses having awareness of your impact on others and how well you operate in relationship with others.

For problem solving to work, the theory states you must generate a range of solutions and use good decision-making skills to enable you to choose the best overall solution.

When teaching EQ, there's an emphasis on these skills as being important in stress reduction and management, by providing a range of solutions and having the ability to determine the root cause of an issue.

Looking at this view, I can see the logic behind it. Surely, when faced with unknown situations, the best thing to do is employ your analytical skills to find numerous possible ways forward. It's a process I've seen and even taught myself over the years.

As we know from earlier in this book, in the world of neuroscience, problem-solving requires a great deal of mental processing energy. It's why so many people struggle to do this effectively, particularly when the brain's energy stores are running low. The reason for the energy depletion is due to the process itself.

Problem-solving requires your mind to not only analyse the current situations, but to find examples of something similar you may have experienced in the past, to enable you to evaluate the best solution. Once again, we come across the desire for us to work from known experiences rather than step into the unknown.

Recently, I've come to place where it feels this really doesn't work or apply to the ever-changing situations we're faced with.

Having a measure of emotional intelligence and strategies to develop more, will not 'fix' these challenges for you, that can only come from within yourself.

AN ALTERNATIVE VIEW OF..... EMOTIONAL INTELLIGENCE

Having a high degree of emotional intelligence is seen by many as a strong indicator of success as a leader or people manager. After all, if you think about the four main quadrants of emotional awareness: empathy, stress management and adaptability, these are features most businesses would assess and develop in their up-and-coming leaders.

However, I began to wonder whether EQ is actually like other models and theories, such as MBTI, and can only offer limited, short term success in dealing with the challenges facing business leaders today.

To help understand the limitations of EQ theory, I will examine a client case of mine. Although he understood the facets of emotional intelligence and the power of logic, he still got stuck in a fearful paralysis.

The client came to me for help in his leadership of people through significant change. He was looking to make changes in the structure and operating model of his department and wanted support to manage the 'people' side of the change process.

The first obstacle he wanted to overcome was what he described as a difficult conversation with a colleague of his. He'd always enjoyed a positive, long-standing relationship with this colleague and by and large they seemed to be on the same wavelength. However, something in the relationship had shifted and he seemed at a loss to know how to tackle this conversation.

The client came to me citing all the leadership development work he had participated in and how he felt he had a great understanding of both his own style and of his impact on others. Yet, somehow, he felt didn't know what to do, to have a successful conversation with this colleague. Between them, they could talk generalities and share mutual observations about the good and bad of the business. There also seemed to be a good level of trust and camaraderie.

The sticking point for my client came about with his proposed focus of this 'difficult conversation'. My client proposed to make large scale structural changes, which would potentially have a big impact on the function of the work his colleague was leading.

My client gathered data and provided the reasoning and logic for the proposed changes. You could say he was using his Human brain to head off any emotional outbursts from his team or his colleagues.

Yet, despite all this 'weaponry', he still found himself stalling, procrastinating and finding endless distractions, all of which provided him with seemingly valid reasons to delay the conversation.

When we talked it through, my client expressed a high degree of fear, that in having the conversation, he would find himself responsible for the breakdown of a perfectly good relationship.

"How do you know this?" I asked.

What emerged were a series of obviously painful experiences where, throughout his life, my client had somehow found himself blamed, shunned or made to feel 'the bad guy' whenever he tried to step into difficult relationship-based situations and move them on.

The result of this was a collection of experiences and associated emotions all stored away in his memory.

In this situation, he now finds himself facing what he fears is another one of those difficult conversations. And, guess what? Both the Chimp and his Human brain, have stepped up, with the intent of providing protection and helping find a safe way ahead. In doing so, all the past experiences, and the difficult emotions associated with them have been brought from his memory into the present.

He became stuck looking at the current need to discuss change with his colleague against a framework of past pain and difficulty.

He asked me to help him find strategies to help him approach the task differently and reach a positive outcome.

I really admired his intent and his deep need to maintain a relationship which was obviously important to him. I could see his bravery in trying to 'do something' to get it right and pave the way to a much easier change process.

It certainly would have been easy to draw on any number of approaches or frameworks to help this conversation happen and move forward.

Somehow though, there was something about this which made me view it differently.

What I could hear in our conversation was the thinking he had created around this situation. His personal thoughts had drawn on the memory bank in an attempt to find a solution.

Of course, what happened actually worked against this process. By looking to past experiences all he did was re-live them and, of course, brought into the present the experience of these unpleasant emotions. He gave them space to expand and magnify.

He reached a point of paralysis, where his thoughts about how the situation could evolve had him firmly looking to the negative. This perpetuated the belief it was not safe to enter the difficult conversation, all created from his own thinking.

What was interesting was to hear him express his uncertainty through what he perceived the actions of others would be. He could quite readily sit and give many examples of anticipated reactions, behaviours and even words, attributed both to his colleague and others in the wider business. The more he created these, the more catastrophic the anticipated outcome seemed to become.

I felt so much compassion for him in this place of turmoil and wanted to show him a different way to approach this situation.

We discussed where these anticipated reactions came from. We talked about how 'true' they were and how much they really existed in his current reality. He readily acknowledged the anticipated reactions weren't quite real as they simply hadn't happened yet. But the emotion he experienced alongside them felt so real, it was impossible for him to move forward.

Naturally, for my client they seemed real, as they were drawn from real reactions and emotions he had experienced in the past. This, however, was the point I made, all of these reactions were exactly that, brought into the present from the past.

I asked him how he thought this was happening and who was doing this. He paused for a moment.

"Well, I'm creating these potential scenarios," he mused.

We discussed how these potential scenarios were in fact coming from his personal thoughts, thoughts he alone was creating.

As a logical man, the chain of thinking started to emerge.

"If I'm creating these thoughts, then I must be creating what I believe the consequences will be."

Exactly.

"Then if these potential consequences are only coming from me, then they are not coming from the people I've attributed them to. They can't because they haven't happened yet, have they?"

He wanted to know how he could counter this well-oiled mind machine which came from his memory.

In this, there was something important to realise. To make this difficult situation work, he had to 'do' very little. We didn't need to talk through difficult conversation drills or various influencing strategies.

All we did was explore the innate understanding and wisdom he already had available to him. I asked him to sit with the possibility he could shift his thinking to a more positive frame. That he could build on the positivity which already existed in his relationship with the colleague and set out to have a discussion which would explore the changes with his colleague, without causing a relationship breakdown.

I helped him see only he was responsible for his emotions and his thinking. No matter what he believed, it was impossible for him to be responsible for or manage the thinking and emotions of others.

Only he could create his thoughts, he could only guess at what his colleague was thinking. I reminded him he had a choice about which of his thoughts to focus on and which he would allow to move through.

I could see there was still a degree of uncertainty. How would he 'know' what to do or say, if he stopped using past events or experiences?

We then explored how all the stored experiences can clutter or fill his head with possibilities, what-ifs and potential outcomes. They create so much noise and take up so much processing power, it led to a real sense of overwhelm.

When it kicks in, it leaves little or no space for anyone to access their own innate intelligence or instincts.

If he was able to let go of the habit of anticipation, managing and controlling, his instinct would naturally show him the way forward. He would find access to a more natural process and outcome.

He looked relieved at this, as if a weight had been lifted from his shoulders and was willing to give it a go.

"After all," he said, "I'm not moving forward right now. I want to set change in motion for the better of this business. Right now the place to start seems to be clear, it's right here with me."

My interaction with this client was a great illustration of the battles we often embark on, simply because we imagine we see things which aren't actually there.

The past experiences, fears about the unknown and speculation about what others might be thinking, leaves so many of us preparing for battles which don't exist.

We take up so much time and energy developing skills, strategies and approaches to deal with perceived battles, in a mistaken belief we can beat the enemy. In effect, when used in this way the emotional intelligence model is providing weapons to fight something which only lives as an illusion in our minds.

No wonder we can become so caught up and ultimately exhausted by these endless, needless battles.

Outside the business environment, there are numerous examples of people who have used alternative principles in working with depressed, anxious and addictive clients and who haven't used any traditional techniques. Instead, they look to a different place to help people 'manage' their emotions.

Let me explain. By holding the view that the way we are, is shaped by our reactions to various external events over our lifetime, misses a vital point.

Those events are not drivers and shapers of who we are. It's the thoughts we create about those events and the way those thoughts were experienced which really created the moment of reality in us.

Going back over past thoughts, emotions and behaviours, really does nothing but take us into another thought-cycle based on events we believe have been "done to us".

If you remember the strong response created by the limbic system in the brain, for survival and protection at all costs, you can see how powerful this thought analysis process is.

The alternative perspective is to turn away from external events as the basis of cause analysis and look inside each person, as the place where thoughts, experiences and subsequent behaviours are created. From this place, each person has a choice to allow a different experience, whenever and however they choose.

For example, by choosing to follow a more intuitive view of an event in the moment, rather than re-visiting old, habitual patterns, stored away in memory, you instantly create a new experience, behaviours and, ultimately, outcome.

Added to this is the amount of processing space or head space opened up when you stop ruminating, analysing and critiquing what has happened. Instead, what you find is more space to experience and respond to an event in a more instinctive, natural and balanced way. In effect, it allows you to align with your core purpose, rather than behind the logic of doing and knowing.

CHAPTER EIGHT:
CHANGING HABITUAL
THINKING

Throughout this book, you'll note how often I refer to our habitual patterns of thought.

Through my work I've come to understand more about my old patterns of thought, my habitual behaviours and where these thoughts and experiences are created.

One thing I've noticed, though, is how even once I 'know' or at the very least become aware of all these habitual patterns, it doesn't 'fix' the problem.

Don't get me wrong, becoming aware is a huge step for anyone. Likewise, being aware and understanding all thoughts come from you and through you is a huge step, too.

Take that awareness a level further and move to the realisation you have the means to access all the wisdom and inner knowing you'll ever need. Well, this is also a massive step.

How is it then that knowing this does not prevent us from falling back into old patterns of thinking?

Why is it, no matter how many theories or models we learn, we still find ourselves acting in the same way we did before the training? I imagine many businesses who invest in a range of training programmes would like to know this, too.

As I write this book, I've noticed how I still get tripped by feelings of fear and insecurity arising from my own thoughts, even when I fully embrace alternative principles.

The key to handling these trip-ups is not to fuel the negative feelings created by these thoughts, with more thoughts and feelings. Getting frustrated, disappointed or judgemental about finding myself back in old, habitual behaviours is pointless, as it only serves to add greater depth to my experience of negative thoughts.

To help understand this phenomenon, I'll go back to my early days as a coach.

Often I'd be asked to help my clients increase their self- awareness through tools like 360 degree feedback. In the process, though, there was always a recognised pattern I used to explain to them.

If, through feedback, they came to understand more about what and how they were operating, leading them to make changes, there would still be some resistance to these changes. This would come either from themselves or even from others around them.

People around you, whilst seemingly relishing your newfound

insight and its positive effects, may feel their own insecurity about what these changes mean to them.

In experiencing insecure thoughts, and their associated feelings, they may well become the very people who aim to push you back to where you were, with the intent to make themselves feel safe.

In a similar way, within each of us, gaining awareness and changing our level of consciousness makes part of our psyche determined to keep things just the way they've always been. After all, it's served you well over the years, why change now?

As a result, changing habitual thought patterns and behaviours is not a linear process. It takes time. It feels like you move two steps forward and one step back, gently nudging old patterns into the past to create the space to embed new ways of being.

The key is to be aware of this and not allow judgements or doubts to kick in. These thoughts only end up undermining the changes you're making.

THE PROBLEM WITH FEEDBACK

It's a difficult situation in business, where over the years, we've been encouraged to give and receive feedback from others as a way to improve ourselves and our relationship with others.

Of course, feedback is simply a vehicle for a person to share his or her thoughts and perceptions of an individual. When you describe the impact a person has on you, what you are actually describing is your own interpretation and reaction to an event or interaction.

It isn't to say it's invalid or untrue. It certainly feels real to the person having the experience.

The misunderstanding around feedback, which I feel has left so many people unsure, insecure and lacking in understanding of steps to take, lies in the source of the feedback.

In reality, feedback is a description of someone's thinking and how this may have triggered behaviours and feelings. These will be and feel completely real for the person experiencing the thoughts. If this person is encouraged to view an event, looking for the less pleasant reaction or experience – they're more likely to focus their thinking on negative perceptions, even if it is veiled in the need to provide 'developmental' feedback.

Anyone receiving feedback can be grateful for the gift of a shared perception or experience. It may serve to raise awareness or insight on how others may be reacting or thinking about their own actions.

Accepting feedback, however, requires an open mind and deep listening. It's a way of creating understanding, compassion and rapport with the feedback giver. Feedback actually gives you an insight into how another person thinks.

If, like the person receiving feedback, you can remain open and curious, then it serves to create more opportunities for positivity than negativity. It really can be a great development tool, beyond its use today.

Right now in business, I believe there's been too much of a shift towards focusing on development gaps or 'weaknesses'. This invokes negativity. It's quite understandable a person receiving feedback may find it difficult to even hear what is being said, let along use it as a tool for creating change.

Feedback, as currently used, has people tethered to a place of inadequacy and reduced self-confidence.

It could offer something so different.

It could, when used in a slightly different way, enable the feedback giver to open the door to positive reinforcing thoughts, which really do become a gift to their receiver. Using noticing and awareness to help.

Noticing is not a constant state. Being aware of the thoughts and habitual behaviours does not suddenly make them go away.

There's a much better way to embed new understanding and let go of old patterns. By not 'trying' or 'working on something', but instead taking our foot off the pedal, we create enough calm and head space to hear exactly the wise thoughts we need.

When we hear this wisdom, our behaviours and feelings will align. It's from here a series of small changes start to happen.

You may not notice each and every one of them because they may individually feel insignificant.

But imagine this... each small change coming from you, as you access your own inner source of wisdom, accumulates over time to create a whole new set of experiences.

CHAPTER NINE:
AN ALTERNATIVE APPROACH
TO... UNDERSTANDING
YOURSELF

Frameworks, such as Emotional Intelligence, Leadership Circle or MBTI, offer a developmental perspective based on change through <u>doing</u> something – something different.

For example, in MBTI you are encouraged to build or develop traits held by those in other dimensions. In other words, if you try to make a positive, extrovert input in a business context and you are naturally introverted, you're encouraged to speak out more spontaneously in meetings, rather than holding back until a thought is fully formed.

Leadership development programmes and most forms of coaching require you to learn, gain insight, and then 'do' something to put the learning into practice in your own world.

In the past, as a coach, I encouraged clients to focus on <u>what</u> action they take between sessions. Now I realise that whilst these clients made some progress by doing something different and creating a change, the whole focus is wrong.

This focus to take action, based on a framework, theory or new process, is once again looking outside yourself to create an experience or an affirmation of change. Having this focus brings in a constant 'top-up' cycle, where you can only feel better and feel you are developing, if you are achieving something outside your own thinking and experience.

For example, if you want to build self-confidence, you may be advised a good way forward is to stand up and share with others your best skills or best qualities.

To achieve this in the moment, you may succeed by taking the step, but the action of public speaking relies on external affirmation. That is, you require others to hear you in order to somehow prove you have gained the self-worth you are trying to develop.

Now as a coach, I take a different direction with clients. Instead of seeking external affirmation, I take people inside themselves, to find the understanding that they can create their own positive thoughts about themselves, just as easily as they have created or become aware of negative thoughts.

This inner resource is ever-present and can be tapped into at any time, with no need for seeking any kind of external reinforcement.

Thoughts of self-confidence sit as readily alongside thoughts of self-doubt.

The shift comes when a person realises they can choose where they place their focus.

They can focus on the negative and perpetuate the feelings associated with these, such as disappointment and sadness. Or they can focus on the positive and notice the shift in feelings which come about, even if the shift is only experienced for a few minutes, initially. It's enough to show what's available whenever it needs to be called upon.

Over the years of exploring these various models with clients, I've experienced in myself enormous shifts in insight and understanding. I've no doubt these eased some of the confusion and misunderstanding I had about myself and others.

Yet, despite all this, I've been in search of the answer to why these models couldn't offer long term clarity or success.

Clients would come to me in a fog of confusion. I knew I could shine a light on their feelings, hold the mirror up to what was going on and help them find some level of insight to move them through their frustration and potential meltdown.

The problem is, I began to realise this momentary clarity and freedom from confusion – whilst glorious as an 'aha' moment – ultimately did not solve the problem.

I'm now able see why.

The use of psychometric tests; the understanding and following of leadership and personal development theories or frameworks; the use of coaching models and techniques, all serve a purpose.

They aim to change thought.

The issue is, they aim to change thought from the wrong place.

We're all so caught up in habitual patterns of thought which manifest as behaviours and beliefs, which feel real and factual. Leadership theories suggest these thoughts can be changed by altering our response to circumstances around us. Giving us the impression that if we become more skilled at managing and responding to these circumstances, we will be more successful.

They come from the illusion we are all subject to the buffeting from the world around us – forcing us to react, respond, protect, and drive through or whatever behaviour we're used to using.

I'm not condemning leadership and development models as worthless or damaging. The models and frameworks I've described were created by people who knew there was something different going on. It was their attempt to make sense and expose what that was.

Myers and Briggs created their preferences model from a place of wisdom and thinking. Through their wisdom they researched, developed and created the model. Their thoughts created their beliefs about how people are 'wired' and how we all operate from different innate preferences and states of being.

What's good about models like these is they serve to change the thoughts and beliefs each person holds about themselves or others.

What's missing in them is something much more fundamental.

Imagine that all your thoughts are not created by external events, circumstances or understanding. What if, they are in fact created from within you?

What if these individual thoughts are simply a manifestation, a guide to a bigger process at work?

Using the image of a boat, your thoughts about yourself and others, are simply a rudder, given to you to steer you along the right path.

What if the process creating that path is driven by something much bigger and powerful than each of us?

This process is the engine of the boat, pushing us through the journey of life and taking us to where our destiny had already prescribed.

Going back to the models, theories and processes, these are magnificent gifts, created to help steer our thoughts. They are designed to open up new perspectives and ways of being more aligned to bring out our true self. None of them are designed to take over the powering of the boat, they simply can't.

Tools like these allow our thinking to change. They move us away from negative, destructive and confrontational thoughts, towards more positive thoughts, where compassion and understanding live. Where we begin to understand our own reality and realise everyone else operates from a place they regard as their own reality.

Having these more positive, healthier thoughts creates changes in behaviours and feelings, as these are both manifestations of what and how we think. If we are in a place where our thoughts are more positive and healthy, if we see and understand more about ourselves and others, we will find our minds are quietened and feel more at peace.

But real, long term change requires more than simply allowing a shift from negative to positive thinking. When we allow thoughts to change, we are allowing ourselves to return to a neutral state.

There are many approaches in the world encouraging us to see everything around us in a positive light. I'm sure you've heard of people who have given up everything in search of a more positive, enlightened state of being: going on retreat, getting closer to 'God' or through extended mediation or periods away at holy sites. These are all ways of trying to bring peace, stillness and positivity which feels like it will shift your very existence.

I'm not saying for a moment there's anything wrong with these positive or enlightened psychologies. However, they don't fully point us in the direction of what's creating our experience and where it's coming from - inside you and through you from the universal power as a whole. These techniques are not designed to be the cause of your change in thinking; only you are the cause of that.

Remember the feeling after that 'aha' moment? It's a sense of relief, a sense of the fog clearing and pressure being released. When you know you have tools to understand, connect and be with others and yourself more easily.

This feeling of peace and quiet opens up the place where you can hear your instincts, where you can notice your intuition and your knowing. When you can tune into this, you're closer to the place where all that you are, is being created.

You let go of the judgement, analysis and self-loathing which made you believe you could never achieve what you set out to.

You have a new understanding which unblocks competing outcomes, you start to unravel the 'facts' or beliefs about yourself and you open the door to finding a new way forward.

You'll start to hear what your instincts are telling you, rather than being clouded by old thought patterns.

You'll know what to do and where to turn next, because all the noise and fuss of goal setting, tracking and failing has been stripped away.

Your inner wisdom will start to show you where to look and what needs to happen to deliver the outcome you're looking for.

Success coach, Michael Neill describes how, in our world today, we follow models based on the belief our experience of life is created from the outside in. It is where we have come to believe people, circumstances or events make us feel something, be it happy, sad, angry or anxious.

To this end, we've spent the last few decades searching for antidotes to these things:

- How can we deal with circumstances better?
- How can we attract the right people to be with us to make us feel complete?
- How we can attract more good things by positive thinking?

In his book, 'The Inside Out Revolution'[16],Neill describes one variation of this model as 'Empowered Outside In' where we believe it's not the circumstances, but what we do in response to them which determines our outcomes.

In this variation, being able to move from being a victim to someone empowered to take on challenges and create positive outcomes, enables us to create the happiness and fulfilment we crave.

Neill then takes it a step further, describing the next variation as 'Enlightened Outside-In'. Here the model acknowledges the importance of circumstances or people creating feelings in us, but the focus shifts to managing what you think about these.

Self-help books, tests and assessments are designed to help measure and understand our thinking, with a view to changing it from negative to positive. If we think negatively about people we are in a relationship with, simply by realising this, and changing it to a more positive position, this will change your experience of that relationship. Maybe over time this will change the people and circumstances too.

The best thing with this model is even if these changes don't come to life, you feel able to cope with a bad situation more easily.

Think about the models and frameworks we've looked at in this book.

Emotional Intelligence is a great model designed to increase your understanding of yourself, your emotions and those of others around you. It certainly adds a lot more to the development of people than simply measuring cognitive intelligence.

I'm sure we've all been with really smart people who consistently fail to see their impact on others and tailor their interactions accordingly.

We've also encountered emotionally intelligent people, who exude a sense of empathy, compassion and grounded understanding of the world of behaviours and emotions.

What's really fascinating is even without Emotional Intelligence as a model and measurement tool, people who are able to show deep compassion and empathy still exist, as do people who remain disconnected from the experiences of others.

The reason for this is simple: we live in a world of thought and these thoughts are created from inside each and every one of us. It leaves us in a place where 'what' others think, and therefore experience, is not as important as understanding this process.

We may still feel uncomfortable feelings around some people or we may feel a great energy boost when we're with others. Those feelings, either good or bad are still only created from inside us, as the experience of the thoughts we have created.

What this means is you don't have to change the world – of others, of circumstances or your own knowledge to change the way you feel. You only need to understand all the feelings you experience have come from thoughts you've created.

It's here so many of us get stuck; I'm certainly familiar with this one.

While we realise we create our thoughts, we're still hooked into the idea that by changing or controlling them, we'll be able to decrease the negative impact of stress or anxiety-causing situations and increase our own sense of well-being. In reality though, we're only halfway there at this point, we're still regarding the underlying situation as the cause of our thoughts, which needs to be managed for us to feel or experience something different.

The way to change your experience is to understand you are always only experiencing your *thinking* about people or events and allow new thinking to emerge without doing a thing.

When you begin to notice these thoughts are there, constantly changing and moving in and out of your life, you can see paying too much attention to each thought burns up far too much energy and space in your thinking.

It's like trying to look at the view from the top of a mountain through a raging blizzard, then getting caught up attempting to look at each and every snowflake.

It's highly likely you'll be exhausted and stressed by trying to lock in the image of each snowflake, which in itself is fast-moving and likely to melt at any moment.

At the same time, the view from the mountain doesn't change; it's still there, but hidden behind the curtain of snowflakes. By chasing the image of each snowflake, you'll miss the big view.

The great thing is you know it's still there as it always is. Once you stop focusing on the snowflakes and start looking through the storm, you'll be able to access the view in all its glory.

In this analogy, you started by thinking of ways to slow down the flakes, of capturing each and every one. And in all likelihood, you'll have experienced a range of feelings associated with this – frustration and disappointment in your inability to contain a flake, or sadness as each flake melts away.

These feelings result from our thinking about the snow storm and the view you know is there. But, while the snowflakes may come and go, you can at any time stop and enjoy the view.

This creates a sense of stepping outside the unpredictability of the storm and focusing on a much stiller, measured place, where changes happen through small shifts in perspective as you stand and take in the view.

PART THREE:
YOU IN RELATIONSHIP
WITH OTHERS

People don't need to be managed, they need to be unleashed.

Richard Florida (2002)

INTRODUCTION

Despite many false starts and removal of this section of the book, I was compelled to write it anyway. Here's why. Development support for relationships in business often only goes as far as team building, stakeholder management or better communication skills. The idea that we are 'in relationship' with others whilst we are working in business is not a commonly explored. To look at overwhelm and meltdown from development interventions based around relationship needs, seemed a step too far. However, it is something not to be ignored, as relationships permeate all business interactions and take up a lot of development focus.

When I first started working with clients, I loved the individual focus. I relished the opportunity to remove the person from external influences and help them gain a new level of insight and understanding about who they are, how they're dealing with challenges and discovering how to find a new way through.

However, increasingly, I noticed these clients always had the same step to take between sessions: having to go back into the wider world and apply what they had learned.

In reality, working with an individual in isolation was a falsehood.

How could they expect to see things differently or make changes, when they were thrust right back into the systems holding them in the same, habitual place, which was comfortable and known?

They didn't operate in a bubble of isolated utopia. They, like all of us, were navigating the realities created by those around them, be it work colleagues, family, friends or strangers. Their interpretation and response (or reaction) to these realities were often as powerful yet unpredictable as the behaviours they were looking to change.

Alongside this realisation, I found myself working in leadership development roles, where team building was becoming a popular activity in leadership development.

I was often struck by the individual nature of this work, designed to focus on building understanding between individuals. But all I could see were events based on psychometric analysis of individuals, using a 'compare and contrast' approach.

What do I mean? Consider Myers Briggs, a popular tool for helping individuals understand themselves, their preferences and how these impact on their own and others' behaviour. What it often did was create a very strong sense of 'us and them' when used to 'build teams'.

I recall one time we used Myers Briggs as a basis of a team building exercise in one senior HR team. I vividly remember being stood in a corner of the room, as 'one of those' development people with a 'feelings' based preferences while the rest of the team stood in the opposite corner, reassured by their sense of togetherness as they all had a 'thinking' preference.

Having people defined by a unique coding or type might help individual insight to some degree. Yet it can create division and complacency in the sense that one type or coding is 'better' or more familiar than another.

With these two experiences in mind, it was a relief when I found a way of looking at teams in a much broader sense. For me, the shift came when I started to explore the idea that work between individuals was based on a systems model. Each part of a team could be viewed as one element in a dynamic, ever-changing system, connected by the relationships between them.

When you look at relationships from this place, you stop the division and see the dynamic, re-balancing nature of relationships. Instead of 'who is doing what to whom', you can look at 'what is trying to happen'.

It's freeing to work on understanding, exposing and watching the relationship between people, instead of pitting one person against another. All of a sudden, the spotlight moves off individuals who perceive they are right or wrong and moves to the essence of the relationship between them.

In doing so, there's a marked shift taking place. Individuals who are part of the relationship are taken away from the place where they are operating blindly from their own view of reality. It removes them from the place so many of us know, where they are governed by what they perceive others think or feel about them, which causes them to react to this perception.

The work of The Center for Right Relationship (CRR)[17] has been at the forefront of this shift. It has brought together learning and approaches from a range of thought leaders and created a strong model for how individuals can operate successfully in relationship with others, be it formally in a team or informally in groups or a partnership.

Through a great deal of research, a number of factors have been identified as essential for the success of teams, globally. The most important factors focus first on creating positivity, the foundation for a range of factors leading to productivity.

Unsurprisingly, one of these core positivity factors is trust.

In the first section we looked at trust in relation to individuals - both self-trust and being trustworthy of others. Even if you believe in your own commitments and your ability to deliver declared outcomes, in a relationship with others they need to believe in you, too.

In this part of the book, we'll continue to look at models, theories and processes describing how best to be in a relationship with others. We'll also explore how those relationships might be enhanced or even found to be unnecessary when a paradigm shift is added to the mix.

This section will move through the following areas:

- Our need to be together
- How others 'make' us feel
- Relationships in teams
- Leading a team
- You in a relationship with others
- The alternative view of relationship development

OUR NEED TO BE TOGETHER

When we look back at the earliest point in our evolution, a strong element in our existence is our need to 'be' and work together. Whilst individually we may have been given tools to ensure our survival, it is intrinsically linked to the need to ensure the survival of the species, as a whole.

The link between us goes way beyond our need to use each other for survival; it's about using the power of the collective to achieve greater outcomes than an individual could alone.

Humans formed tribes, hunted together and formed communities to tend to children, animals and share living arrangements.

This need to be together has changed in form over the years. Industrialisation moved people from disorganised, chaotic ways of working to the development of production lines and mechanistic processes. Each part of the working process was intrinsic to the overall performance, resulting in little or no space for difference, creativity and new ideas.

It created the command and control leadership models, many of us are still familiar with today. Leaders held the position where whatever they said was to be done, without question, by the lower order of employees. The notion of inspiration, setting direction and sharing the future to build alignments was a long way from this way of operating.

At this time, innovation, creativity and decision-making developed in spite of the system, rather than through the system. Today, leading others and creating the environment with these essential factors looks completely different.

Steven Jobs did not create Apple's success by stifling creativity or dictating only one way forward. His approach to creativity and decision-making enabled great ideas to bubble to the surface and moved them from idea to execution in the shortest time possible.

Later in this section, we'll look more closely at his approach which threw away any vestiges of command and control and what it means for adaptability in leaders today.

CHAPTER ONE:
HOW OTHERS 'MAKE' US FEEL

People in any kind of relationship with anyone else - as a boss, work mate, employee or customer - typically hold the belief these relationships govern how they feel at any one time. Often, we attribute so much of our sense of well-being, or unease, to what others have done to make us feel a certain way.

What if, for example, your boss continually checks on your work, offering corrections and feedback on how you could improve it?

For most capable, self-sufficient people, if this happened daily, you would expect a reaction as follows:

"I wish my boss would leave me alone. His constant checking is so annoying and makes me want to scream in frustration. I wish he'd understand how he makes me feel and how much better work would be if he gave me some space."

Whilst you might say this, at some level you know your boss and his behaviours don't make you want to scream. You want to scream because of the feelings his actions create in you.

The same applies when a relationship generates some positive reactions:

"I've just solved a really tricky problem for a customer and she was so grateful. It was so good to help her, she made me feel really useful. It's made my day!"

You can see how we give the behaviours of others, the power to make us feel and act in a certain way.

Do their behaviours really have this power?

If so, do you need to manage their behaviours to get the feelings we want?

When you think about developing capabilities, such as influencing techniques or customer service skills, they are often based on the concept you can manage others' behaviour to obtain a positive outcome. After all, if you learn to use a range of influencing styles you'll be able to somehow manage and control the behaviours of others. Maybe you'll even change their view or approach to something. Right?

If this were the case, why are so many business people left struggling to manage the behaviours of others and striving to maintain good relationships with those around us? Not only this, why does this management and control not deliver the good feelings we thought we'd get?

It's easy to see why so much team development training, focused on managing differences and creating techniques to control reactions, has limited effect. Think about it, when has anyone been able to change your behaviours for a sustained period?

Trying to eradicate difference and manage reactions will not work for teams. The response to control or forced change from most people is to push against those forces. What you get as a result is more disruption, conflict and disharmony.

No wonder businesses struggle to get the best from teams and the development road can be frustrating at best, or destructive at worst.

Why is this?

Earlier in this book I described some truths which form a new perspective on how we operate in the world.

In the example above, your experience of the interfering manager is not created by what the manager does or doesn't do. Instead, it is based on the thoughts you have created about your manager. Those thoughts become your experience through consciousness and are entirely owned by you.

When you describe the feelings associated with interactions you have with the manager, they have been created as part of your experience. We know such negative thoughts, fuelled by our focus, tend to multiply and gain strength as we hand them more power and energy.

Given you create your thoughts and create your own version of reality, you are in control over the power you give them. You don't need to change your thinking, try to be more positive or even try not to think (as if you could!). It's about the amount of energy you put into believing the illusion...after all, it just comes from thoughts, right?

With so many of our thoughts coming from our personal, habitual thinking, we can become stuck believing the same 'reality' over and over again. In this way, it really does look and feel like our experience of others comes from who they are and how they behave. It's where you so often hear: *"He (or she) makes me feel this way"*.

Here's the shift.

When we realise we create our thoughts and experience, we see the behaviours of others around us also come from their own thoughts and consciousness. Believing we can understand or interpret thoughts in others is foolhardy. In reality, we only see the world around us through our own lens of thoughts, not others.

We're so conditioned to view others by how similar or different they are to us, we perceive them to be thinking the same thoughts. It can't be the case, as you create your own unique thoughts and experiences in your own way. In this way, no one can make you feel something. You will only feel something created by your own thinking.

If you can understand your feelings - as coming from your own thoughts - you can reclaim your ability to allow different thoughts to replace old thinking at any time and follow those which bring balance and positivity. By understanding these simple truths, you can see you're not the embodiment of others' thinking. You only represent your own.

In the case of the 'interfering manager' you may be wondering how to change this situation.

One approach would be to separate yourself from this manager's experience of their reality and pull back from blame, criticism and judgement, allowing more space in your own mind. Instead of thinking up strategies of attack or self-protection, start to consider how your boss may be thinking. Don't do this because you need to understand more or solve their problem, simply notice the impact of the different thoughts each of you are creating.

By using deep listening - and by that I mean, *really* listening and suspending your need to action your own thoughts - you'll move closer to understanding the reality of others.

MY REALITY: OUR REALITY

Whatever is going on with us as individuals, can be applied to relationships with others.

In the first part of this book I looked at traditional approaches in the on-going search to know yourself better and understand yourself more fully.

The analysis and self-analysis so many models and frameworks offer promise to help you understand more. It can go astray; when, in finding out more about yourself you become more self-critical, ignore your strengths and focus instead on what needs to be 'fixed'.

Furthermore, in reality, during each day, minute or hour you're also impacted by your moods. When we shift into a low mood, these elements can look huge, even catastrophic and keep us in a negative place. You create a new 'reality' reinforcing the need to stay low, until all these problems are 'fixed'. In itself, this perpetuates a low mood state and the view we hold about ourselves or others.

In teams or indeed any kind of relationship, it's important to realise the impact of individual thought and experiencing of thoughts, when people come together in a group.

How you think about yourself may be so all-consuming as an individual which leaves you unable to see the shared experience that we all have with each other. Expanding the view from 'me and I' to encompass 'us and the whole system' moves the relationship into a much broader "what's really happening here" perspective.

As a result, whenever people connect, they bring their own thoughts, their own experiences of these thoughts and the different relationships they have created.

ALL VOICES TO BE HEARD

In the model created by the Center of Right Relationship[17], they suggest a powerful mindset or tool to be used in groups to encourage everyone to listen deeply to every perspective. It is called Deep Democracy, where all voices are given express permission to be heard, even if they hold non-aligned views.

It's not as crazy as it sounds.

How many times have you been in a meeting - even with only a few participants attending - where it's clear no-one is listening to anyone around them?

At a certain level, they may be trying to hear others' words, but often these words are crowded out by the thoughts filling the head space of each individual.

If you consider the training time and focus spent on developing listening skills, it demonstrates its importance to successful human relationships.

The mere fact each person in the room is really only listening through the lens of their own thoughts and experience of these thoughts, shows us it's a skill which needs more work to understand and use successfully.

No wonder teams, groups and partnerships run the risk of misunderstanding, conflict and disruption, where people do not feel heard, unconditionally, or without judgement. Deep listening, alongside Deep Democracy, is clearly the way forward.

How many leadership assessments and frameworks truly reflect these two sides of the 'all voices to be heard' coin?

In most businesses, there's a great reliance on 360° feedback, where opinions of others are used to help us understand how we relate to each other. By its very nature, though, 360° feedback is coloured by the thoughts and experiences of the person giving the feedback.

That's not to say feedback is wrong, as it will provide a snapshot of thinking and experiences in the moment. But it cannot objectively reflect the thinking or experiences of the person receiving the feedback, nor their intentions or their version of reality.

What people hear or receive as feedback and what people experience as a member of a team (or in any relationship) are all driven by one simple fact:

Every event, situation, piece of information, presented to people will be viewed through a projection of their own thoughts.

If you look at a relationship from this place, it's clear to see why misunderstandings and conflicts occur. When individual thinking is vastly out of kilter or misunderstood by others, the same event looks very different.

CHAPTER TWO:
RELATIONSHIPS IN TEAMS

WHAT IS A TEAM?

A team is a group of individuals coming together with a shared purpose or task.

A team may be made up of only two people and may not even be labelled a team. It may be called a work group, project group, working party or business partnership. Its label doesn't matter. What matters is it aims to perform something more than an individual may achieve alone.

Katzenbach and Douglas in their 1992 article, *The Wisdom of Teams: Creating the High Performance Organisation* (Harvard Business School Press)[18], take a narrower view. They define a team as:

"A small number of people with complementary skills, who are committed to a common purpose, performance goals and approach for which they hold themselves mutually accountable"

The implications behind this definition are that teams can be any size. However, if a team is too large it will naturally form sub-teams to facilitate logistics of meeting, sharing information and building relationships.

It's clear that diversity of talent is an important component, as long as team members are drawn together to enable success in achieving a common purpose and goal. A common approach signifies a need for shared rules and behaviours. Having clear roles within a team underpins a common approach, as roles help define how skills, talents and activities are divided for success.

Katzenbach and Douglas argue groups of individuals must move through a range of stages before they can be regarded as even having some potential as a team, let alone becoming a high-performing team.

They describe how groups of individuals evolve from simply being part of a working group, through to becoming a high-performing team over time. These stages are described as follows:

> ### Formation of a working group

A working group represents a collection of individuals where sharing of information and best practice is carried out, with the purpose of helping individuals perform tasks better.

> ### Creation of a pseudo-team

The group may evolve into a pseudo-team, where there is an opportunity for improved performance through collective action. This is often not established or achieved at this stage, so people continue to act in individual best performance rather than collectively.

This type of relationship grouping is the most troublesome for organisations, as the façade of a team exists. It can be disconcerting to find the performance just isn't present and, at this stage, even individual performance can slip. It can be a high risk state.

➢ Becoming a potential team

The next developmental phase is where the group becomes a potential team, with concerted effort to develop a greater collective purpose; to develop more shared approaches to working; to clarify roles and to achieve a level of shared performance. The key focus is to create a sense of shared accountability to drive the shift from individual to team.

These teams are found throughout businesses and it's often at this stage team coaches are drafted in to help the team leader get some of these essential building blocks 'over the line'.

➢ Formation of a 'real team'

The next phase is when the group starts operating as a 'real team'. Here, shared accountability has been established and the team has a shared commitment to achieve common goals. This is what Katzenbach refers to as a basic unit of performance.

It only becomes a high-performing team when the collective focus shifts to ensuring each other's personal growth and success - not to the exclusion of others, but for the improvement and success of all.

The development process doesn't end there. In this section, I'll take a closer look at the positivity factors needed to create a high-performing team and how these lead to increased productivity.

TRADITIONAL TEAM DEVELOPMENT

When I started in the business world, I was taught teams should be developed as a set of individuals.

We applied awareness-raising tools, such as MBTI or Insights, (as we reviewed earlier in this book), to these individuals and carried out a 'compare and contrast' exercise across all of them. Each team member was encouraged to view their uniqueness as someone with a 'Yellow' profile or having INFP preferences, and compare their understanding of these types with others.

Based on these, the team development approaches concentrated on bringing together our understanding of each preference, style or type, adding in adjustments and adaptations, to enable each team member understand others in relation to their own assessment.

There was value in gaining an understanding of others and why or how they behaved as they did. The downside was the application of labels. To me, these created a differentiation, leading to greater risk of separation, rather than bringing people together.

In addition, none of these models offer true, instinctive understanding of what drives people to be the way they are.

The models offer insight on how and why things work the way they do, but they do not shed any light on the principles which lie behind how people think and how they experience their lives.

Many times, I would see and hear people in team building events disclaim ownership of what they had or hadn't done, due to their type label.

For example, I'd hear:

"I'm not comfortable making the presentation, as I have a high introversion preference. We need to give the task to a team member who is more of an extroverted person, as they'll find it easy."

Or:

"I'm a 'blue' type. I work much better with data than people, so no wonder I find team leadership a challenge."

To me, these labels could so easily become a hindrance in people coming together and really understanding who they were and how they could work together effectively. Tying people down to labels or types has always felt like a constraint, even if, initially, people feel more able to understand each other better.

When you apply these limitations within a business, there's a risk of limiting performance instead of enhancing it, as the development programme would aim to do. Multiply this phenomenon across multiple teams and business meltdown becomes a real possibility.

WHAT MAKES A TEAM WORK?

I've been lucky enough to do a lot of excellent training in how teams work and how to help teams work better.

When I needed to move beyond the traditional approach to teams and team building, I looked at the work of the Center for Right Relationship (CRR), created by Marita Fridjhon and Faith Fuller. Through Fridjhon and Fuller, I was first introduced to the concept of teams being living and dynamic systems, rather than collections of individuals held in a static pattern with each other.

Their model of relationships built on work by: Daniel Goleman (Emotional Intelligence), which we've explored earlier in this book; John Gottman, who spent decades researching and supporting sustainable relationships; and Arnold Mindell, who provided much of the groundwork for systems thinking in relation to human relationships.

The systems approach to working with teams represents a fundamental shift away from examining interactions at an individual level to a more powerful place, where the relationship between team members is where change happens.

In the systems approach, if you change the relationship between individuals in the team, you'll change the team.

In addition, by being part of a team, relationships will have an impact on each individual, through the culture and behaviours created by those relationships.

In similar work by Team Coaching International (TCI)[19], they explain this clearly in their four guiding principles they believe underpins all teams. These are:

- Teams exist to produce results
- The team is a living system
- Team members want to be high performing and want to produce results
- The team has within it the means to excel

What these principles indicate is the innate capability available to all teams when members recognise what is shaping their experience of circumstances or events around them. It also shows, as with all parts of nature, how teams are innately able to find balance and equilibrium and adjust to change.

There's a solid base to develop further understanding of what makes teams more successful. Researchers identified collections of behaviours and mindsets found to create a positive state for team members, leading to higher levels of success and productivity.

FACTORS NEEDED TO CREATE A HIGH-PERFORMING TEAM

Through extensive research by Marcus Buckingham and the Gallup organisation, there is a clear indication that all relationships, whether business or personal, flourish when the pervading behaviours are positive rather than negative.

The work by Gallup consistently describes how people are still more likely to leave an organisation due to the breakdown of relationships (with a boss or team) than due to the job itself.

Experiencing negative behaviour erodes relationships to the point where it's preferable to move on rather than try changing them. Later in this section, we'll take a closer look at what happens when relationships break down and how they can be recovered.

John Gottman[20] has carried out some great work in defining what makes relationships function and what causes them to fall apart.

His description of the 'four horsemen' toxic behaviours offers a robust model to understand negative behaviours and how they can erode a relationship if allowed to run unchecked.

Gottman even created a positivity ratio which he believed supported a successful relationship, that being: 5:1 positive interactions over negative. We'll look at this in more detail below.

When toxic and negative interactions dominate, we see an erosion in some of the core constituents of positive relationships. The positivity factors are defined by TCI are as follows:

Optimism: people are inspired by a shared vision for the relationship and activities of the team or partnership. They are able to see the contribution of all and create energy in working together for a common outcome. This factor negates toxic behaviours, such as a cynicism, as well as the sense of hopelessness created through a focus on experiences from the past.

Trust: you'll by now know how important trust is in all relationships. Trust can be judged by how willing people are to share views and feelings, without fearing others will respond badly. Trust and trustworthiness are seen in people's ability to deliver what they commit to do.

Respect: having a positive view of each other and removing any sense of contempt or hostility towards others. This sits closely alongside trust and is a strong antidote to toxic behaviours.

Communication: the focus of many leadership development programmes. In broad terms, in any relationship, communication is as much about listening as talking. Ensuring communication is open and directed at the relevant parties minimises the level of gossip or stonewalling toxic behaviours present.

Constructive Interaction: focusing on the mindset necessary for dealing with disagreement as a positive force rather than something to be feared, controlled and managed. Blame, criticism and defensive behaviours are to be minimised, creating more space to hear and understand another person's position.

Camaraderie: having a sense of belonging together as a team or partnership, allowing all team members to share jokes, have fun and develop empathy for one another.

Values Diversity: the celebration of all the talents, differences and personalities which come together to form a team. Building on respect and trust in the differences present, provides all a team needs.

Having these factors does not happen as a constant state. I'm sure you recognise times when a team seems to have all the factors which come together to form a good relationship. As with any system, however, it's always in a state of flux and can easily move from a positive to a negative state. A shift in any one of the factors causes a ripple effect and, of course, may trigger toxic behaviours, which in turn further erode positivity within the relationship.

WHY POSITIVITY?

Daniel Goleman and his team describe the role of the emotionally intelligent leader in creating positivity:

"......the fundamental task of leaders is to prime good feeling in those they lead. That occurs when a leader creates resonance – a reservoir of positivity that frees the best in people..."

How does positivity free the best in people?

In his research on relationships, Gottman cited positivity as an accurate predictor of the success or failure of any relationship. This is supported by Goleman's work on the development of emotional intelligence.

Emotional intelligence can only exist when people are in a relationship with each other and is essential for such relationships to be successful. Any relationship system needs a high degree of emotional intelligence, to achieve the best results possible.

While much team development centres on what happens when some or all of these factors change, there's less understanding of what causes these factors to change.

For example, trust. As described earlier, you're able to offer trust freely and ask from others, if you can demonstrate trustworthy behaviours.

To give trust in any relationship, you start with a default position which is trusting someone until you are given reason to do otherwise. Occasionally, you may encounter a moment on initially meeting where something about an individual triggers a slightly alarming, 'don't trust this person' reaction.

It is likely to be caused by your emotional centre (the Chimp), having a fear-based, past-memory moment, where you drop into defence mode or see someone as a threat. Of course, as Steven Peters suggests, the best way to deal with this is access some 'human mind' management and apply logic, evidence based thinking to offset the impact of emotion.

I suggest a different approach. What we experience in these early relationship moments is not the person who we have just met. We are actually experiencing our thoughts about the person. These thoughts are drawn from our emotional thinking stores or more logical thinking frameworks. Either way, the experience of others comes from inside each of us through our individual thinking.

How can you really know someone is a threat when you've never met the before? Try not to follow thoughts drawn from your personal reference frameworks. Instead allow space to access your inner wisdom, which will show the true nature of what the relationship could be.

With the dynamic nature of relationships, you can only imagine how much of this inconsistent thinking occurs in every individual in the team or relationship.

For many in this field, there is a strong correlation made between the presence of positivity factors and the ability of the team to achieve the outcomes they're looking for - in other words, their productivity. In the productivity factors defined by Team Coaching International, you can see the building blocks of true team development laid out by Katzenbach and Douglas.

These factors are:

Goals and strategies: where the team are clear on the goals and objectives to be achieved and how they will be rewarded and recognised for doing so. Goals are aligned to overall business strategy and its plans, so the teams' efforts clearly contribute back to the business.

Alignment: not just in goals and strategy, but creating a strong common purpose within the team where the members collectively own their results. The behaviours supporting this are co-operation, collaboration and cohesion. With alignment, the team becomes a strong unit.

Accountability: each team member understands his or her role and what is expected from the role. In this mutual accountability framework, all team members understand the consequences and follow-up which will happen if an individual fails to maintain an agreed standard.

Resources: this factor focuses on sharing the resources or talents available to the team. Sharing is seen the benefit for all, rather than the success of an individual over others. This factor strongly correlates with valuing diversity and positivity factors.

Decision-making: the team creates and maintains effective decision-making processes. I've looked at this more closely when I examine how decision-making works and how common business behaviours can block effective decisions being made and solutions being found.

Proactivity: this factor focuses on the team's ability to anticipate and respond to change. This approach helps the team see change as a positive and necessary part of its evolution and the business, rather than something to be resisted.

Team Leadership: this is more than having a nominated role described as a team leader. It's about each team member stepping up and offering leadership whenever necessary and for any leader role to be fully supportive of the team as a whole.

These factors underpin business performance and are constantly the focus of development interventions. Achieving the creation of a 'high performing team' is the goal of many leaders and development specialists.

The belief is this will create outcomes and success through the collective skills of the team.

CHAPTER THREE:
LEADING A TEAM

Reading this as a business owner or leader in a larger organisation, it's likely you'll be wondering how all this plays out in your role as a leader.

When you realise people rely on you for direction, for answers and for problem solving, there's a moment of understanding of the power you hold over them. When I realised this, it was a moment of horror. I had recruited all the members of the team and my direct reports were all hugely experienced and capable in their areas of expertise.

I had deliberately recruited people who were better than me in a number of specialisms. I wanted to be surrounded by talent and felt my role was to guide, shape and direct this talent for the best outcomes.

That's not to say it's easy to do this. On the contrary:

Have you ever sat in team meeting and looked around at the expectant faces and thought, "what am I supposed to do now?'

I have and it's a genuine moment of insecurity with a dose of paralysis thrown in.

If I knew then what I know now, I would have felt something completely different.

From my perspective, there are two routes to take as a leader of others.

Imagine everyone in your team is a uniquely coloured and shaped balloon, full of potential and trying to rise to a height and place unique to each balloon. Each balloon has a beautiful silk cord trailing below it and each cord is available to be picked up and held by whatever team and organisation the person drifts into.

You, as a leader, hold those silk cords every time you bring them into your team.

Now here's the thing: how you hold those cords impacts on how well you capitalise on the uniqueness of each of those balloons.

If you hold them too tightly and twist them together, you will find a lot of energy is taken by each balloon, hitting, bashing and tussling with one another in a very tight space. You'll find the talents held within each will be lost in those battles. You'll find each balloon becomes slightly deflated and loses the perfectly-balanced bounce it started with.

The other way of holding those beautiful cords is to create a space where the cords are in your palm, but are free to play out, to extend beyond others, to bob and weave as needed in the moment. Releasing each balloon releases the talent, the potential and the uniqueness in each and every one of them.

You will notice energy is created, rather than used up. You will know each of these balloons, held in a gentle way, will be free to flourish and deliver all they are supposed to.

You will no longer feel paralysis or the fear of what you should do with them – they will dance and bob, just as they need to. Each will have the space to float freely and the energy-draining 'bashing' up against other balloons simply won't exist.

You can call this many things in terms of team leadership and development. It's about creating the space for people in your team to be what they are, having them unconstrained by your own insecurities or fears. Having a loose grip gives a place of anchor we look for in others, yet allows enough space to work and focus on exactly what will work for the good of the whole.

LETTING GO

If, like me, you have had years of training in how to be a leader, the general perception is that to lead and manage others effectively, you have to keep a tight grip on what they do, how they perform and what they create.

Look at the appraisal and performance management systems in most organisations. These provide rigid frameworks within which a manager and employee have conversations about past performance and future targets. The format can even extend into behavioural ratings, to give a clear and consistent measure on how an employee has carried out their work.

Now, I know from experience, these systems come from the right place; as they attempt to add consistency and objectivity to what are basically subjective perceptions about individuals. Add to this, the need to assign a reward or bonus, based on ratings, and you can see why these systems have moved towards becoming pseudo-scientific.

For me, the issue with these systems is they are fundamentally based on lack of trust.

They have been created because there is a fear management are so influenced by their personal, subjective perceptions, they must be given rigorous guidelines within which to operate.

Similarly, on the other side, you have the notion employees cannot be trusted. Having them provide 'evidence' of their performance and feedback from colleagues or customers indicates, to me, just how disconnected we have become as businesses and employees.

To re-establish a connection I believe we need to do the opposite from the current trend of tighter and tighter managed systems.

We need to let go.

In the first section of this book, we explored letting go in the context of you, as an individual. This focused on letting go of trying to control and manage the huge amount of external variables, to allow a more free-flowing, healthy process of thinking to flow through you.

What I suggest here follows the same principle. As a leader or manager of others, you need to realise both you and your employees have the in-built capacity to create all you need, when you need it, in a way that works perfectly with you and others around you.

I'm not suggesting you create a complete free-for-all in your business, allowing everyone to come and go as they please or doing exactly what they want.

There's plenty of space to create a container within which your employees will settle.

The container is a sense of purpose for your business, the intrinsic values permeating how your business operates and feels to others and the need or purpose of the products or services your business sells.

When a container is there, the best thing you can do is make sure you have the people who align with what your business offers and therefore, encourages them to be part of it - not simply earning money from it.

Imagine knowing each of your employees has the innate skills, capability and willingness to deliver *exactly* what your business needs.

The questions you're probably wrestling with right now may include:

How do I do that?

How do I let go and ensure my people will be committed to delivering results for me and my business?

'Letting go' sits right next to 'doing nothing' in the answer to these questions.

It might involve a change in focus and decision about where your energy goes. Where you should now be looking is towards the need to engage, build relationships and listen to each and every one of your employees.

In my experience, this doesn't easily happen in businesses because people struggle with insecurity, fear and ego, where the belief is, they need to have the answers, solutions and tasks every minute of every day to take care of every possible situation.

I remember this myself, having a team member come to me and feeling I needed to provide the answer right then and there. It was fairly overwhelming to wake up each day with this expectation. I came close to my own personal meltdown.

What it also meant was in the moment, I couldn't really *hear* what my member of staff was saying. I can still remember the feeling of scouring my memory banks to find a similar situation as a way of guiding me to the answer. Knowing what I do now, I realise how unnecessary this was.

All I had to do was listen, *really* listen and hear what innate wisdom was available to me and members of my team to find the right way forward.

Looking back to past situations was not the answer, as it was likely to take me back to past mistakes. Had I been able to relax, trust in my inner wisdom and be ready to use the talents available, it would have resulted in expending less energy, creating less stress and anxiety but creating more solutions.

Of course, what the frantic thinking actually did was guide me away from really listening and made me recycle the same thoughts, centred on managing and thinking I needed to control my external circumstances to change my feelings

This kind of response has two effects. It shuts down access to the natural process within you, where you could more easily tap into the innate wisdom you have ready.

The other effect is the constraint placed on your team member. They will have been hooked into your habitual patterns of thinking and will find their own channel of natural creativity blocked. It will take a leap of faith for a team leader to step back and stop driving through externally constructed processes.

What if you were innately tuned into what the people in your team needed?

What if you stopped long enough to actually hear what people on your team had to say?

What if you really understood the talents of each person on your team?

This is what will happen if you embrace the truths about how our world works. When you notice and embrace your own inner wisdom, your instinct, you create the space for developing a way forward. You create the right actions but more naturally and in balance with everyone in the team.

Equally, if you are leading a team and notice conflict developing between two team members, a few routes are available to you.

You may try direct conflict resolution, or you might find yourself siding with one of the team, whose views feel more like your own.

What would be most valuable is to encourage both team members to see how they are creating the situation by their thoughts, usually based on what has happened in the past. Remember, how the brain creates mental maps from experiences and past events.

We use these maps to help inform our personal thinking and to try to make sense of current situations. By helping them look to a different place of who is doing the creating, rather than what is being created, they will realise they are creating the experience of conflict and therefore they can allow that experience to shift.

Using some of the work from the CRR, it's possible to bring two people in conflict to a place of mutual respect, deep listening and understanding of what's trying to be achieved. This occurs even if resolution looks like 'agreeing to disagree', which becomes possible when individuals find the space to decrease the impact of their negative feelings towards each other.

DECISION-MAKING IN TEAMS

I referred to Steven Jobs earlier in this book, as a supporter of accessing intuition to create and innovate.

He believed teams, especially large groups, made the best decisions and developed the best products, but only when leveraged correctly. This is why he favoured demo units and other physical objects for visual aids rather than slides on a screen, as Jobs felt these tools got people more engaged.

According to Jobs, the purpose of a meeting was to:

"Get people talking about it (the idea), argue with people about it, get ideas moving among that group of 100 people ... and just explore things."

Here's something that Jobs once said to the journalist Walt Mossberg:

"If you want to hire great people and have them stay working for you, you have to let them make a lot of decisions and you have to, be run by ideas, not hierarchy. The best ideas have to win, otherwise good people don't stay."

Making a smart decision has to be more important than who makes the decision. Only then is the 'right' decision the one that pushes forward the ideas, not the person who said them.

In short, Jobs relied on his gut as the primary guide to his decisions. He sometimes let others win arguments, but it was because he himself decided their ideas were better.

He doesn't seem to have ever reached the point of making decision-making a team sport. He did not aim to integrate a range of perspectives, simply to form a consensus-led course of action.

Granted, there is some evidence even Jobs came to realise the shortcomings of one man's intuition as the only source of decision making.

After returning to Apple for the second time, there was a change in Jobs. He started to rely on others, listening more and trusting members of his design and business teams.

It didn't signify a move to consensus decision-making, though. He still held the single point of accountability as the way to make decisions and to change them if a better solution was on offer.

He remained true to his instincts and his role as a leader.

CHANGE IN RELATIONSHIPS AND TEAMS

When you look at relationships, what you see are a collection of thoughts, generated from individual perspectives. If you consider each person in a team views the world, events and others from their own perspective, it's clear to see why people often misconnect.

Starting with the individual, each one creates a thought from inside themselves. It either comes from their inner reservoir of innate knowledge and instinct (if there's enough stillness to hear the messages) or they create thought from a memory or from a mindset they currently hold.

Whatever the source, these thoughts create a unique perspective through which the person filters and interprets events around them.

Relate this to the traditional view of team. It is a collection of individuals, who are all different and yet are all, somehow, expected to align, collaborate and perform well together. No wonder this expectation presents a challenge to most teams.

If every member of a team reacts to external events, as seen through their own lens and experienced as a series of feeling or behaviours, this leads to the creation of constrained and negative thinking.

No wonder there is a strain and conflict. You really can see the concept of 'who's doing what to whom' here.

No-one in this way of thinking / feeling, having sourced their filter from personal thought, can create enough space to truly hear or understand any other perspective.

Even if team members attempt to share their perspective, it's highly unlikely anyone else in the team will actually be able to hear. They will be listening for words, behaviours or feelings, which will serve to affirm their perspective or create a defensive reaction to enable them to protect their "reality".

To me, interventions designed to facilitate change in a team are working on the wrong part of the process.

If we hold onto the understanding that, in an individual, change only comes when an individual changes their understanding on where thought is created and becomes aware of their own natural insights, surely the same applies to the collective of a team of individuals? When a team focuses their energy and thoughts on managing, controlling or reacting to external events, what do you end up with?

You will find an array of thoughts, feelings and behaviours - which may feel aligned (fighting the same cause or fighting the same enemy) - yet this is likely to be short term in nature.

Very soon, individuals refer back to their own version of reality, seen through their own lens and created by their own personal thought. The variation and breadth of scope of each of these versions of reality show how easy it would be for a team to fragment, contradict and fall into conflict behaviours.

It would be a different scenario if team members understood they were creating their own version of reality, and not to negate this but to find access to a more natural process of experiencing change.

Being able to respond to an external event with collective understanding of the power to create thought and associated feelings/behaviours is the first step.

Each person in the team would be less hooked on holding their version of reality and would be open to understanding others from a more expansive perspective.

In a team possessing this understanding of where thought comes from, positively responding to change becomes easier. This occurs even if the response is to simply be present, to notice and enjoy every moment, positively embracing the collective power of the team rather than feeding negative or destructive thoughts.

CHAPTER FOUR:
EMOTION IN RELATIONSHIPS

To be in a relationship with others uses thought and awareness to fully experience the connection we have created. There is always emotion in relationships, be it experienced as positive or negative, by everyone involved.

The CRR describe relationships as a flowing river, with rapids, smooth sections, swamps and whirlpools, all providing a vast array of possible experiences. Over time, as our life brings us into contact with a part of the 'river' we find difficult or uncomfortable, we move from seeing relationships as vast and full of possibility, to being something constrained and narrowing down our willingness to experience all that is on offer.

Initially this narrowing down feels as if we've moved into safer waters, but in the long term, all it does is dull down our relationship potential. It makes us stick more rigidly to the emotions and behaviours we are comfortable with, for fear of re-visiting others we've known, but perhaps have disliked or misjudged.

In the CRR models of relationship development, they advocate coaching and developing the relationship between individuals, not the individuals themselves. They hold the relationship comes from a deep place within us and its natural unfolding will bring about trust, reduce resistance and develop the natural way forward.

In their view, "every feeling, expression, or behaviour within a relationship is a message, the beginning of something trying to happen".

Through coaching, CRR aims to stay in the present moment and enable a deeper experience of the moment, rather than entering a prolonged and deep analysis of past events. This comes from the belief that right in every moment lies the wisdom needed to grow and change as the relationship needs to.

What the CRR team point to is the way all relationships inherently have the capacity to find balance and equilibrium, if they are allowed to do so. This capacity comes from inner wisdom existing in each individual in a relationship, and also within the relationship as an entity in its own right.

What's missing in many relationships today is not this wisdom. It's the awareness each individual has about the wisdom available to them and the relationship.

I've seen this at work in the mediation work I do.

In the course of mediated conversations, you hear a person attributing blame to the other, for example saying: "you are more manipulative than you think".

A disagreement is likely to arise when the other person denies this is the case. Their denial, is not that they're lying, it's more likely they have no awareness of their behaviours and the impact on others.

Telling the individual, explaining why and how it presents itself will not lead to him or her suddenly gaining awareness. Instead, to gain awareness the person has to experience it, not hear or think about it.

This will raise his or her level of consciousness (awareness) and provide a new route to make change possible, fuelled by more wisdom from within him or herself.

It may be the individual accused of being manipulative, has pushed this part of them to a deeper self, as they are uncomfortable with it or find it associated with certain emotions they don't want to experience. If you struggle with manipulative behaviours in yourself, you're more likely to be sensitive to or less tolerant of it in others. It can get to the point where you project on to others what you can't bear about yourself.

When this happens, I often ask my clients a very simple question:

If you are accusing someone else in a relationship of having an issue with anger, ask yourself what is the 2% truth is for you.

In other words, if only 2% of what they've observed in others were to be found in themselves, what would it look like?

It makes the experience of a marginalised emotion more palatable than asking them to own the anger they have tried to submerge.

As we've seen earlier, no amount of control or external techniques will force someone to change how they feel or behave, until they themselves access their own insight. The issue with relationships is, these emotions and subsequent behaviours are magnified and often reinforced by interactions with others.

Often, the impact of emotion in a relationship becomes so embedded, negative and destructive behaviours are created. That's when a relationship starts to fail.

RELATIONSHIP BREAKDOWN

TEAM TOXINS

Despite all these attempts at establishing and maintaining control of others, even with the best intentions there are many occasions where a group of people coming together creates nothing but adversarial exchanges, heated arguments and personal attacks. Some will react with aggression and defence, while others will remove themselves from the situation by going quiet or leaving the room.

Here's an example:

I was once asked to work with a team who were disenfranchised from their organisation. The team members were very vocal about the changes going on around them and many were openly obstructive towards the management team. I worked with them for several sessions, gently uncovering their levels of dissatisfaction, the main areas of their discontent and how far these views permeated within the team.

It became clear the overall mood of the team was stuck firmly in the negative. There were a couple of dominant voices who were determined to drive home their perspective and have the rest of the group rally round them in agreement, all against the enemy - the management.

The behaviours and negativity present in each meeting were so destructive and attacking in nature, it really felt there would be no moving on. I decided to try something different.

I educated the group about 'team toxins' or the four horsemen of the apocalypse, as they are described by their creator, John Gottman. He is well-known in his field of marriage and relationship counselling and much of his research centred on marital relationships.

Gottman says in many relationships, the deterioration will take place when both parties start to generate and use some of these toxic behaviours. When they appear, they tend to do so in a specific order:

> **Criticism**

> **Contempt**

> **Defensiveness**

> **Stonewalling**

Criticism:

What's the different between a complaint and a criticism?

Complaints only address a specific action which the other person in relationship has carried out or failed to carry out.

e.g. *"I'm really angry you didn't clean the floor last night, we agreed to take turns."*

A criticism is more 'global, all encompassing', where you might add in negative words about another person's character or personality

e.g. *"Why you are so forgetful? I'm always having to sweep the floor when it's your turn. You just don't care."*

This horseman is very common in relationships.

The problem with criticism is when it continues is it pervades a relationship – it leads to a far more toxic horseman...

Contempt:

Contempt is shown by a range of behaviours, such as sarcasm and cynicism, plus:

name calling; eye rolling; sneering; mockery; hostile humour; even appearing to assume the high moral ground.

Contempt is fuelled by long-simmering negative thoughts about the other person. It's likely these thoughts will arise if differences are not resolved.

In whatever form it shows up, contempt is very poisonous to a relationship as it conveys a strong sense of disgust.

This makes it hard, if not impossible, to resolve an issue if others in the relationship perceive you are disgusted with him or her. Therefore, contempt typically leads to more conflict rather than reconciliation.

A close cousin of contempt is belligerence, which is just as deadly. Belligerence takes the form of aggressive anger because it contains a threat or provocation, which you'll know it when you hear:

"Well, what are you going to do about it?"

Unsurprisingly, the next horseman to appear in response to this perceived risk of attack is:

Defensiveness:

Unfortunately, defending yourself from attack doesn't usually help the conflict to end. In fact, just the opposite happens, as it escalates the conflict. Defensiveness is really another form of attack:

"It's not me, it's you"

Just a note - these three horsemen don't always gallop in the same order. They can often arrive like a relay match, handing the baton off repeatedly.

When this builds, you will often find one person will 'tune out', heralding the arrival of the fourth horseman:

Stonewalling:

Stonewalling is when someone turns away from conflict, reduces their interaction and simply stops responding. Here a person will stop the non-verbal listening cues and look away, look down and utter no sound. It may seem the person is acting as if they couldn't care less about what you're saying, even if he or she hears it.

It's common to see refusal to engage, withdrawal and the silent treatment. At this time, the first three horsemen become so overwhelming, stonewalling becomes a way out.

HOW TO CHANGE NEGATIVE INTERACTIONS

These interactions are based on a build-up of habitual responses. They are often linked with some behaviours and emotions we are trying to avoid.

To break the pattern Gottman recommends the following:

1. Increase awareness in yourself
2. Notice when a toxic behaviour appears and agree to move on without it
3. If it has already got a hold of you, take a break before aiming to start the 'fight'

4. Use different ways to communicate

Noticing and naming toxins, without blame or analysis is a great first step. Alongside this, though, is something even more powerful. To counter the toxins, naming and expressing awareness of strengths and the contribution of others, provides a strong antidote.

Expressing the strengths and talents of others is rare in all parts of our lives. Too often, we are taught to focus on weaknesses or areas which are lacking. This makes us believe something is wrong and needs to be 'fixed'. Even with the use of feedback, we find it harder to give and receive positive feedback. It's almost as if we're waiting for the 'bad news', the real message about what's wrong or not good enough.

When I had a senior development role in a large corporate organisation, much of the focus was in assessing and categorising talent at different levels in the organisation. I remember having endless disagreements with external 'experts' who insisted the focus had to be on identifying and correcting areas of weakness in these populations.

I came from a different place. I believed there was more value to be added by developing, enhancing and freeing up the strengths and talents of people across the organisation. For me, having people entering a process of assessment, feedback and development planning should create the outcome of discovering their true skills and the motivators needed to release their talent in the organisation.

Have you have noticed the resistance and denial that emerges when people are asked to focus on their weaknesses and areas of concern, with no counter balance from areas of strength?

By shifting the focus to a more positive developmental approach, it helps move away from any toxic behaviours.

Remember when we looked at the impact of 'chimp' in individuals and how it aims to protect and sustain the survival of the individual and the species.

Well, guess what? Put a team together and you're likely to see a whole range of 'chimp' based reactions emerging, if the collective focus is on weakness and negatives. After all, there's nothing more threatening to the ego than being exposed for what it cannot do. It's not surprising these toxic behaviours emerge as a reaction to the perception of being attacked.

Added to this, people in a team blame their feelings on others, believing they are being 'made to' feel a certain way due to the actions and behaviours of others. With this belief, every member of the team puts responsibility for they are feeling on circumstances outside themselves. They feel unable to change – waiting for the world around them to change instead.

No wonder teams or anyone in a relationship with another person, would habitually react with blame or criticism, or by trying to side-line an opinion through stonewalling.

When you look at the well-researched factors which create strong relationships in teams or any other structure, you see how factors such as trust, optimism and respect are all essential. With these in place, there's little room for the toxins to take hold. Finding constructive ways to disagree and still reach decisions takes the pressure off individuals and allows the natural relationship balance to be maintained.

Unfortunately, sometimes these factors are eroded by a series of toxic interactions. It's then that the relationship needs help to repair.

REPAIRING RELATIONSHIPS

Start from this place:

"We don't experience money, we experience our thinking about money"

Apply this to conflicts or problems in any relationship.

In all likelihood, you've been in a relationship as it erodes and gradually breaks down to such an extent it seems unlikely any repair is possible.

Gottman's range of 'team toxins', show the power of some behaviours when these problems occur.

I've been brought in many times to mediate or work with 'broken teams'. It quickly becomes clear that toxic, often destructive behaviours come from very negative, fearful and aggressive thoughts held by different parties in the group.

The solution to the root cause of the problem or relationship breakdown doesn't lie in finding and addressing the problem. Nor does it lie to trying to correct, control or change behaviours of people in the group. It lies in the understanding the problem isn't real - it's only something created by the thoughts of the people involved.

Most certainly the feelings experienced are felt and real, which may cause strong physiological reactions in those experiencing them. In turn, the person experiencing these feelings will create more thoughts about that experience.

The solution lies in the knowing that these feelings are created by the thinking of people involved.

The problem in a relationship does not come from a circumstance causing negative thoughts or toxins; it is only your belief in the thoughts about the issue which cause you to experience the problem.

Moment by moment, thoughts are created, float in and will float out again without effort or focus if this is what the individual chooses. Know that in the next moment a new thought will replace it. It's really that simple.

Relationship repair would become less necessary if individuals became aware of this process, when you can step back and not be drawn into a cycle of destructive thoughts. Taking ownership of your thoughts, experiences and choosing a calmer path is available to everyone.

MEDIATION PROCESS FOR RELATIONSHIP BREAKDOWN

Sometimes in my work as a coach, I'm asked to work with two parties in an organisation, where their ability to work together - or even be together - has broken down.

The mediation process illustrates the breakdown in the core elements of a relationship, which are then magnified and further disrupted by each individual's thinking about the situation.

In this process, I see each party in the mediation separately at the start of the process. It gives them a chance to tell their story and to feel heard. It allows me to establish a relationship with each of them, through creating an environment of trust, understanding, deep listening and rapport. All of these positive foundations are necessary in developing a successful relationship.

In listening to each person, you hear their story and their experience based on their thoughts, emotions and behaviours.

What always strikes me is in so many of these 'broken' relationships, each party perceives the problem as being with the other. I hear them recount in great detail how the other person sees a situation, how they must be thinking and why they have acted the way they have. How do they know what the other person is really thinking?

People become so entrenched in the notion they have done all they can and if only the other person could see their point of view and make changes, all difficulties would be resolved. Once again, putting the solution to the 'problem' outside themselves, to be fixed by others.

Does this sound familiar?

I recommend a different perspective. When working on re-building a work relationship, I use certain techniques, such as finding points of alignment and highlighting where both people already agree to re-build trust and negate perceptions they may hold. Just this step has often changed people from being cautious, reserved and defensive to being relaxed, laughing and more open... and even being in the same room as the other person.

This hasn't happened because of anything they or I have done. What has shifted are the thoughts they are focusing on. All I have done is pointed them in the direction of finding alignment and rediscovering places of positivity. Once this process begins it's much easier to shift more of their thinking towards a positive outcome.

However, this isn't always enough. The real breakthrough occurs when each person starts to see they misunderstood what was happening. This happens when we discuss the notion of where thought, behaviour, feelings are coming from in the first place. The realisation dawns that resolution doesn't lie in them driving changes in the other person. Change and resolution comes when they understand their thoughts are creating their experience. They are not responding to the behaviours or actions of others, they are responding to the thoughts they have created about those actions and behaviours.

This understanding puts both parties in a much better place to resolve their immediate differences and arms them with all they need to head off future issues.

It's clear people are always going to experience the same event differently and may fall back into the belief that this experience has been caused by others. Once you understand any experience is only based on your own thought, you can more readily go back to your own choices and allow that experience to change too.

FORGIVENESS IN RELATIONSHIPS

Taking relationship repair further, consider this:

All love, forgiveness and compassion comes from a thought.

They are positives from thought and will attract more love, compassion and forgiveness in your life.

If you can fill a relationship with thoughts of negativity, expressing feelings of hostility, anger and frustration, you will fill your experience of the relationship with those feelings.

If you can raise awareness by revisiting past pain and negative thought, you will only heighten the pain and negativity and bring it into the present. Such experiences need to remain in the past where they were experienced.

It's not about denying they happened. It's about not bringing them into the present, to recycle and strengthen.

Finding space in thought to allow forgiveness and love will, in turn, create greater space. It reduces judgements of ourselves and others and allows us to forgive insecurities and fears which may have created certain behaviours.

Our inner wisdom allows us to access love and forgiveness in abundance. There is no need to try as it is already there, waiting for us to remember and invite us in.

Being in a relationship with others, where you see them with love and compassion, opens up a space for them to be who they truly are and feel held with love.

CHAPTER FIVE:
THE ALTERNATIVE APPROACH
TO.... YOU IN RELATIONSHIP
WITH OTHERS

If you remember in the first section of this book, we explored a different paradigm at work, which will naturally provide balance and create effortless solutions when needed.

The three principles within this paradigm describe some fundamental truths about our world, these being:

1. We are alive and the (formless) life force that powers us has innate intelligence
2. We create thought, which is there to provide guidance and steer our way through our lives
3. We experience thought through our level of consciousness (what we feel)

As principles, they exist in the world around us, even if we are not aware of them. In the same way, gravity, is a principle or truth that has always existed, even before it was named, understood and measured. These principles describe a natural process running through each and every one of us. When we allow this process to flow, the highs and lows of life will come and go. We have the power to access all the answers we might be looking for, in dealing with all parts of life. It's easier to do this when we create the space to hear our inner knowing, hear what it is telling us and trust enough to relax and let the natural process work in its own way.

Obviously, it's important to know this process as something that happens to each individual. That said, like all things, we don't operate in isolation.

As humans, we are wired to build relationships with others. In fact, we are all innately connected to every other human, even if at times we feel worlds apart.

When we look at how people relate to each other, it's important to start from a different place than many of the frameworks I've described.

These traditional models and frameworks, though useful, focus on the outside in world, the world where people react to what's going on around them, to what they believe another person has 'done to them'. This new paradigm is hinged on the opposite truth, where the world we see and experience is created from inside each and every one of us. In this respect, we have no real understanding of what or how others experience the same issue. We can only ever report on how we see and experience it.

What we believe to be true about an experience is in fact only an illusion, created by our thoughts, which leads to feelings and certain behaviours.

When we are experiencing something, we are only experiencing our own thoughts and emotions associated with it. These may have been drawn from past experiences, knowledge and analysis. When we work too hard at examining our thoughts, we're very likely to be drawn into an energy-draining cycle, which fills our heads with judgement, guilt, blame and more. Ideally, we would be able to clear enough space to experience thought derived from our inner knowing, from the instinctive understanding of what's happening and the unfolding of what to do next.

If this is what happens with each individual, imagine what happens when they come together as a group or a team. I've been involved in working with teams who are part of large-scale change in a business. The typical processes I've used centre on exploring key areas of how the team fits into the business, how it is led, how processes support the team and how clear objectives and goals will affect them.

Moving away from typical change management approaches, I work with the group to have them write down their thoughts and experiences of these processes. What I've noticed is how helpful they find this kind of exercise as it gives a voice to some of the frustrations and unspoken beliefs about what the change issues might mean to them.

The problem is you obtain a lot of different perceptions of the same issues. As a facilitator, it's easy to get caught up in some process of trying to rank, categorise or attempt to address every one of these perspectives.

I've come to realise this process whilst surfacing issues and concerns about proposed changes, actually only serves to take people down a route created from past experiences, analysis and personal views. In doing so it amplifies the belief an unpleasant event is being 'done to them', as it has always been seen in the past.

For many, the change itself is not the issue; what creates resistance are the fears associated with it.

How about we look in a different direction?

Imagine these fears can be removed simply by each individual letting go and realising they are the only ones creating that experience. Therefore, they have complete control over how they feel, react and behave. Imagine too that by letting go, removing the analysis and over-thinking, more space is created for each individual's inner wisdom to come to the surface, as instinct or intuition.

How does this play out in teams?

If you are the leader of a team or function, you might be unknowingly governed by your personal thoughts, which if coming from the place of ego and past experiences, may create emotions such as anxiety or fear.

These thoughts are likely to have you gripping very tightly to establish some kind of control, after all that's what you've been trained to do right? You need to establish goals, you need to create alignment and you need to track progress, all because of your personal thoughts which tell you that's what's required to manage others.

You've been taught that in development programmes and watched others do the same. The fear is, if you don't, you will fail as a leader. You will have a team all acting for their own benefit and pulling in different directions. In fact, your thinking would have you believe, without control and management, chaos will ensue. Of course, you are trained and developed, to 'get it right' as a leader and you have all the tools at your disposal to do that.

Creating a shift in how successful you are as a leader is based on something completely different. Whatever your role in a team, a big change in interaction and outcomes can occur very simply.

In going into a meeting or even just a conversation with others, do so with an element of detachment. Let go of the need to be 'right'; 'know more'; 'to have to lead the way' and of the need to work hard to find solutions, as we are generally trained to do.

These ways of thinking are more aligned to your ego, which requires you to appear to be something in the eyes of others. When you let go of this, you can come into a relationship exchange without attachment to your agenda, your view of the right outcome or your thoughts of other's agendas.

Take a few moments to really notice where everyone is: What's the tone of the meeting or the call? What's the unspoken 'temperature' in the relationship? Is it warm, cold or frosty? As questions are posed, with solutions or answers debated, take a few minutes to ask yourself, "what is trying to happen?" rather than tracking whose view or approach is 'better', than someone else's.

Quieten your personal mind to listen deeply and create the space for others around you to do the same. Notice the pauses between speaking, the space between thoughts and resist the temptation to fill or analyse with your own personal thinking.

Of course, you can only do this for yourself and it's not your role to force others to do the same. When you come from this place, you'll find others naturally follow your example, because they will see something completely different in how you behave and the results you achieve.

PART FOUR:
STOPPING MELTDOWN

If you do not change direction, you may end
up where you are heading.

Lao Tzu

WHERE ARE YOU HEADING?

In this book, you've only had a glimpse at the ways in which
you are caught up in a development cycle, which is taking you
nowhere.

Every tool, technique, method and theory aims in some way, to
change your behaviours to make you 'better' at something.

Some of these models follow the route of awareness-raising.
Some look at how past events have shaped your world today,
delving into the experiences and memories, in an attempt to make
sense of how you behave and what you understand.

Some measure, analyse and try to predict your behaviours, based on vast amounts of data and comparisons with thousands of others, 'like you'.

I believe, every one of these was created in an attempt to help; to find the answer; to make you a better person and be able to deal with more of life's challenges.

The issue is, they are all based on a misunderstanding. One which causes more confusion, overwhelm and stress than the challenges they are trying to fix.

At its simplest this misunderstanding has us looking for the 'answer' in the wrong place.

Each one of these theories or models tries to create a route for you to have a better life, more success as a leader and better business performance. They look to changing your behaviours and understanding motivations behind behaviours.

In his book, *The Missing Link*[21], Sydney Banks makes an interesting observation:

'Orginally, psychology examined the connection between mind and soul, until that theory was abandoned. When psychologists stopped investigating the connection between mind and soul, they lost two of the most important clues to what they sought.

They focused instead on behaviour, leading us away from our true psychological nature, ultimately encouraging us as passive victims of life'.

To Banks, the emergence of techniques and therapies focused on behaviours, which moved us from understanding how to find our own inner wisdom. Instead, we are encouraged to follow the beliefs of others, crafted into a model or theory. In doing so, we become followers, replacing our own beliefs with those of others, which may cause a temporary sense of relief, a feeling that the 'answer' has been found. However, a permanent, authentic realisation can only be found through accessing our own inner wisdom.

Banks saw that there were Three Principles, which would explain the whole range of human behaviour and feeling states, all of which create the 'human experience'. These are:

1. Mind: is the energy and intelligence of all life, whether in a form or formless. The Universal Mind, or the impersonal mind is constant and unchangeable. The personal mind is in a perpetual state of change.

2. Thought: is the divine gift, which serves us immediately after we are born. It is the creative agent we use to direct us through life. It is our rudder to steer us through life.

3. Consciousness: is the gift of awareness, it allows the recognition of form... form being an expression of Thought.

Every thought, emotion and behaviour that has and will ever occur, can be explained by these Three Principles. When you believe your thoughts come about as a result of your feelings, you are looking in the wrong direction. Just as you are when you believe circumstances or events in life cause you to think or feel a certain way.

What's really happening is you are experiencing feelings in response to your personal thoughts. Often this clouded, cluttered thinking, serves as a warning that you are blocking the natural processes for maintaining balance. In doing so, you'll respond to emotion-led thinking and will be unable to hear the instincts which would bring you back into balance. In doing so, you are interfering with your natural well-being and access to your inner wisdom.

It's clear these principles describe how our experience of life works, not a way to 'live life'. They don't promise a happy and stress-free life. They do not tell you how to 'fix' yourself or others.

The principles describe the process behind the on-going flow of life we create, a description of how we operate as humans, whether we are aware of it or not. With these you have a framework to help you understand how your life is created through thought. In this, your thoughts don't need to be managed or changed, in the way some models explain. With this understanding, you realise that you allow your experience of life to move through you and you allow your thoughts to change, with the ebb and flow of the naturally re-balancing system in which you operate.

All this comes from within us.

Layering techniques, processes and activities designed to bring change, only serves to block the system. When you feel the system get stuck, it's so easy to push harder, to force your way through to the 'right answer'. That's when you begin to feel overwhelmed, frustrated and 'out of kilter'. Working your way through a day may start to feel like a battle of 'should / ought to / must do'. There is no natural flow to this state.

Replicate this over a number of people in one business and you will find unclear thinking, lack of creativity and lower levels of resilience. Your people will put more energy in trying to work against perceived obstacles than they use in clearing a way forward.

THE NATURAL SYSTEM

You'll have noticed at points in this book, I refer to a 'life' system, which has a natural balance and equilibrium, when we allow it to flow freely.

I'm aware this concept may be a little difficult to understand, so I wanted to explain it using an example from nature.

In every season of the year, the plants and animals around us live out their existence in line with natural processes.

Take for example birds. They migrate; return; build nests and hatch their young in naturally occurring patterns. These patterns are inherently designed to ensure their well-being and the continued survival of the species.

These patterns aren't rigid. When conditions around them change, birds adjust and respond accordingly. If the winter is harsh, or the spring arrives late, or the summer is dry, birds will adjust their behaviours in response. They may nest later, they may migrate earlier or look to find different food sources.

These adjustment doesn't happen because they've looked up a book, or found a new source of knowledge. They happen instinctively, as the birds allow changes in nature's system to change how they respond.

As humans, we are all part of the same natural system. The flow of universal energy, which connects us to every other living being on the planet.

What's different for us is this – we have the gifts of Thought, Consciousness and Universal Mind. Syd Banks explained that the Universal Mind represents part of the much larger system formed of universal life force, energy, or spiritual power, which runs through our entire existence. When left to move us freely through the system, these gifts allow us to respond to the variances of life with the understanding that the system will naturally re-balance and protect our innate well-being.

However, unlike our fellow creatures in nature, we also have the capacity to block the system. Our personal thinking creates experiences which we see as problems and answers yet to be needed.

My fears of business meltdown came from my personal thoughts and experiences. I can see the effects of external methods, which try to create change in each of us. It's something that I see places an unnecessary strain on us and I believe blocks the fulfilment of potential in each of us.

Understanding what's possible <u>when</u> we allow the natural system to work, made it imperative for me to write this book.

I don't want to see any individual or business investing more time and money in finding solutions in the wrong place. I don't want to see any more people become more overwhelmed when they 'fail' to change. I don't want to see talented individuals bogged down with processes or techniques which take them away from their natural state.

Instead, I want to see businesses and leaders let go of 'doing more' and 'knowing more', to allow them to embrace what already exists inside each of them.

FURTHER DISCUSSION

I didn't write this book to negate the work of researchers, theorists and thought leaders.

I wrote this book to start a conversation, to encourage debate. I want people to understand there is a different way and its' here already, just waiting for us to notice.

If you have been touched by anything you've read or you're curious to understand more, let's continue the conversation.

If you don't agree or feel frustrated by the words I've written, that's fine too, let's continue the conversation.

My ultimate aim for each and every one of us to understand and access our full potential. This is how I believe you can do this, once and for all.

FOOTNOTES /REFERENCES:

1. Steven Peters, The Chimp Paradox: The Mind Management Programme for Success, Confidence and Happiness, 2012, Vermilion

2. David Rock, Your Brain at Work 2009, Harper Business

3. Stephen M.R. Covey, The Speed Of Trust, 2006, Simon & Schuster

4. Stephen R. Covey, The Seven Habits of Highly Effective People, 1992, Simon & Schuster

5. John P. Kotter, Leading Change, 1996, Harvard Business Press

6. Kurt Z. Lewin, psychologist (1890-1947)

7. Philip Goodwin & Tony Page, From Hippos to Gazelles, 2008, British Council

8. Robert Kegan and Lisa L. Lahey, Immunity To Change, 2009, Harvard Business Press

9. Myers-Briggs Type Indicator

10. Insights Discovery model

11. Occupational Personality Questionnaire

12. The Leadership Circle, Bob Anderson

13. Jason Fried and David Heinemeier Hansson, ReWork, 2010, Vermilion

14. Mooji, Before I am, 2012, Mooji Media

15. Damian Mark Smyth, Do Nothing!, 2012, 3P Publishing

16. Michael Neill, The Inside-Out Revolution, Hay House

17. Center For Right Relationship, www.centerforrightrelationship.com

18. Jon R. Katzenbach and Douglas K. Smith, The Wisdom of Teams,2002, Harper-Collins

19. Team Coaching International, www.teamcoachinginternational.com

20. John Gottman, The Seven Principles of Making Marriage Work, 1999

21. Sydney Banks, The Missing Link

NOTES:

NOTES:

NOTES:

NOTES:

NOTES: